*Susanna Moodie:* A LIFE

Jamie & Karen,

   This is to commemorate
your own adventure
"roughing it in the bush"
of Dunedin —
   Don't forget Susanna
and her husband moved
back to town, too!

                    Andy
                       Sept 11, 10

# *Susanna Moodie:*
# A LIFE

There is something in my character
which always leads me to extremes.
— Susanna Moodie

## Michael Peterman

ECW PRESS

The publication of *Susanna Moodie: A Life* has been
generously supported by The Canada Council, the
Ontario Arts Council, and the Government of Canada
through the Book Publishing Industry Development Program.

CANADIAN CATALOGUING IN PUBLICATION DATA

Peterman, Michael A., 1942-
Susanna Moodie : a life

ISBN 1-55022-318-6

1. Moodie, Susanna, 1803-1885. — Biography. 2. Authors,
Canadian (English) — 19th century — Biography.*
1. Title.

PS8426.063Z8284 1999    C813'.3   C98-931380-8
PR9199.2.M65Z8284 1999

Cover design by Guylaine Régimbald.
Imaging by ECW Type & Art, Oakville, Ontario.
Printed by AGMV l'Imprimeur, Cap-Saint-Ignace, Québec.

Distributed by General Distribution Services,
325 Humber College Blvd., Etobicoke, Ontario M9W 7C3.

Published by ECW PRESS,
2120 Queen Street East, Suite 200,
Toronto, Ontario M4E 1E2.

www.ecw.ca/press

PRINTED AND BOUND IN CANADA

# TABLE OF CONTENTS

*Introduction:* Passages from an Eventful Life ....... 7

*Chapter 1:* The English Years, 1803-32 .......... 21

*Chapter 2:* Rough Years in the Backwoods, 1832-39 61

*Chapter 3:* Belleville and Its Perils ............. 119

*Chapter 4:* Conclusion — Alone Again ........ 167

Works Cited ..................... 175

# INTRODUCTION:
## *Passages from an Eventful Life*

The land of our adoption claims
Our highest powers — our firmest trust —
May future ages blend our names
With hers, when we shall sleep in dust.
Land of our sons! — last-born of earth,
A mighty nation nurtures thee;
The first in moral power and worth —
Long mayst thou boast her sovereignty!

Union is strength, while round the boughs
Of thine own lofty maple-tree
The threefold wreath of Britain flows,
Twined with the graceful *fleur-de-lis*;
A chaplet wreathed mid smiles and tears,
In which all hues of glory blend;
Long may it bloom for future years,
And vigour to thy weakness lend.

With these lines, Susanna Moodie set the mood for the first
chapter of *Life in the Clearings versus the Bush* (1853), her
sequel to her first Canadian book, *Roughing It in the Bush; or,*

*Life in Canada* (1852). Effusive yet cautious, the epigraph is
a hymn to Canada's future strength, a strength rooted in the
twining of Britain and France as wreaths wound tightly
around the "lofty maple-tree." However, being an English-
woman to the core, Moodie leaves no doubt that, of Canada's
two founding nations, Britain, "[t]he first in moral power and
worth," is the major nurturing power. As such, she implies a
second union, the twining of herself as emigrant, as "daughter by adoption" (*Life* 280), with Canada, the "land of our
adoption." She offers her "highest powers" and "firmest
trust" as models to others.

The optimism of Susanna Moodie's vision of Canada was
nothing if not excessive, especially for 1852-53. Nevertheless,
it was as the spokesperson for Canada's future that Moodie
sought to see herself, despite the fact that she could draw
upon only a limited set of experiences in Upper Canada: to
some extent, it was a role that had been chosen for her at that
point in time. In the autumn of 1852, when she started to
write *Life in the Clearings versus the Bush*, she was nearly
fifty years old. *Roughing It in the Bush* had made her a celebrity and had extended her confidence, even though a few
Canadian newspaper editors heaped abuse upon her for her
negative views of Canada and the Irish. At the same time,
she was just recovering from a life-threatening illness, and,
with the resurgence of her physical strength, she seems to
have resolved to put herself forward as a national and cultural
spokesperson, even though Canada was still far from nation-
hood. Encouraged by her English publisher, she wanted
above all to bring out more clearly the positive aspects of
her Canadian vision that critics of *Roughing It in the Bush*
had conspicuously chosen to overlook in their attacks on
her. Gone would be the melancholy of that book, though
Moodie declared that she would not stoop to flattery, "servile
adulation," or personal dishonesty in order to "gain the

Susanna Strickland Moodie, c. 1850.

PHOTOGRAPH BY G. STAUNTON, TORONTO.
COURTESY MISS KATHLEEN MCMUSSICH.

approbation of the Canadian public" (*Life* 277). No longer regarding herself as a sorrowing "alien on [Canadian] shores," she would focus her attention upon Canada's "pleasant and rapidly-improving society" and its future prospects, dedicating herself and her family to that future (280, 276). She did continue to grumble about what she regarded as wilful misunderstandings of *Roughing It in the Bush* and the low state of literary culture in the country, but overall she sought to be emphatically positive.

In retrospect, there is no doubt that Susanna Moodie did succeed in "blend[ing]" her name with Canada's. The best of her prose writing about the country has been a staple for Canadian literary scholars and cultural historians of succeeding generations. Interestingly, however, it is her "melancholy" first book about emigration and pioneering that has established itself as one of Canadian literature's most cited, analysed, and debated nineteenth-century texts (*Life* [xxix]). As one astute early commentator remarked, one can no more leave Hamlet out of Shakespeare's play than omit Moodie and *Roughing It in the Bush* from the discussion of letters in Canada. When one considers that this statement appeared in the Peterborough *Daily Examiner* on 25 July 1885, a time when only the venturesome would have written so confidently about a phenomenon called Canadian literature, it seems all the more prescient (see "Poets").

In this century, no early Canadian writer has surfaced so often as Moodie in the novels, plays, and poems of important English Canadian writers. Arguably as well, no nineteenth-century Canadian author can match the quantity of critical commentary that she and her famous book have received. Much has rightly been made of the importance of Haliburton's Sam Slick sketches, John Richardson's *Wacousta*, and Catharine Parr Traill's literary record, to name a few rivals for critical attention, but the sheer volume of response to

Moodie and *Roughing It in the Bush* is an inescapable fact. With that broadly based cultural and literary consequence in mind, I shall attempt in this monograph to describe who Susanna Moodie was and how she came — albeit briefly — to assume the role of cultural spokesperson in the growing but still insecure and politically vicious world of midcentury colonial Canada.

The way in which Moodie achieved this position is fascinating. On the one hand, she earned it by writing *Roughing It in the Bush*, a book that made her an international figure, popular and much praised in Britain and the United States. In the process, however, she became known to many in Canada as the apostle of negative views about the country and a necessary target for rebuttal. She was labelled many things. Charles Lindsey, the son-in-law of William Lyon Mackenzie, called her "an ape of the aristocracy" and *Roughing It in the Bush* "a most mischievous [novel]" (qtd. in Thompson 203). While some accused her of Canada-bashing, pro-Irish editors chastised her for her attacks on Ireland and Irish character. Her support of reform principles in the 1840s led conservatives to question her loyalty to Britain and to characterize her as a dangerous republican.

On the other hand, even as Moodie assessed various hostile Canadian reactions to *Roughing It in the Bush*, she was willing to take on the role of spokesperson for colonial Canada. She would raise her head high and attempt to overlook the colony/country's competing voices, its multiple anxieties, and the nastiness of its party-based or religion-directed newspapers (which were virtually the only forms of sustained journalistic expression available) in order to be Canada's apologist, its praise-singer. Her aim was naïve. Perhaps, however, it was necessary — for herself as a person who felt that she had sacrificed much to the land of her adoption (in particular, her own youth and two of her children) and as a

writer for whom patriotism was a vital passion, and for a
colony/country that seemed to her much in need of a rallying
cry. No doubt she also hoped it would generate better Canadian press for her work. But though she wanted to be liked
and respected, she was too proud and candid about her own
experiences to be less than forthright in her opinions. Moreover, she was fully convinced that her own experiences were
valid guides to interpretation.

Being a cultural spokesperson was a role that Moodie
soon found impossible to fill. Her writer's skin was too thin,
she was too susceptible to bruising at the hands of editors
and critics, and her memory of past wrongs was acute and
unforgiving. She could not, she discovered, escape the long
shadow cast by *Roughing It in the Bush*. It followed her
implacably and she was usually judged in terms of that book.
By 1856, she had had enough of serving as the convenient
target of Canadian newspaper editors. Writing to her English
publisher that summer, she vented her accumulated frustration:

It is difficult to write a work of fiction, placing the
scene in Canada, without rousing up the whole country
against me. Whatever locality I chose, the people
would insist, that my characters were *really* natives of
the place. That I had a malicious motive in shewing
them up, and every local idiom I made use of, to render
such characters true to nature, would be considered a
national insult. You don't know the touchy nature of
the people. Vindictive, treacherous and dishonest, they
always impute to your words and actions the worst
motives, and no abuse is too coarse to express in their
public journals, their hatred and defiance. Have I not
already run the gauntlet with them? Will they ever
forgive me for writing *Roughing It*? They know that it
was the truth, but have I not been a mark for every

vulgar editor of a village journal, throughout the length
and breadth of the land to hurl a stone at, and point
out as the enemy to Canada. Had I gained a fortune by
that book, it would have been dearly earned by the
constant annoyance I have experienced since its publication. If I write about this country again, it shall never
be published till my head is under the sod. (*Susanna
Moodie* 169-70)

She was true to her word. Tendering, as it were, her resignation as cultural spokeswoman to English editor Richard
Bentley, she was not long in abandoning her writing career.
Turning to the painting of floral arrangements as a modest
means of income, she wrote very little thereafter, never again
regaining the momentum of and enthusiasm for literary
expression that had carried her through the 1840s and most
of the 1850s.
   Were Susanna Moodie able to speak to us from the bus
in which Margaret Atwood situates her in the final poem in
*The Journals of Susanna Moodie* (1970), she would no doubt
express her amazement and gratification at the level of prominence she has achieved in the years since her death. One
part of her sensibility, a very strong part, craved literary
recognition and praise. Likely, however, she would be very
disappointed to find that readers in Britain and America,
where she was first lionized for *Roughing It in the Bush*, have
shown so little interest in her achievements as a writer since
that time. The neglect of British literary scholars would no
doubt be for her a particular sore point. At the same time,
she would be puzzled, bothered, and offended by much that
has been written about her. She held strong personal views
that she felt compelled to express, especially in her autobiographical writing, and as the preceding passage vividly
reveals, she was pricklish and inconsolable when those views

aroused hostility and disfavour among the pundits of her adopted land. As well, the very invasion of her privacy involved in a biographical study such as this would probably arouse her Victorian rancour, even though the best of her writing is autobiographical and remarkably self-revealing.

The record and shape of Moodie's experiences in nineteenth-century Canada, where she lived from September 1832 until her death in 1885, are essential in two ways I have already hinted at: first, in attempting to understand what was involved in emigrating as a gentlewoman to Upper Canada in the early nineteenth century and trying to make a life here; and second, in seeking to investigate the conditions and problems facing the writer (or artist) in Canada during colonial times. It is certainly not unreasonable to see Susanna Moodie as a typical English gentlewoman put to the test by "Canadian" and northern realities — abruptly removed from the comforts of her rural Suffolk life, the protections of her middle-class family and friends, and her personal aspiration to succeed as a London "bluestocking," only to be exposed without sufficient preparation and training to the rough and demanding experiences of pioneering in frontier Canada. Careful readers of *Roughing It in the Bush* will be familiar with the many variations upon this theme that Moodie plays in the book.

There is, however, more to Moodie than the cliché of the unwilling, long-suffering, and (for some readers) "bitchy" pioneer. To be sure, she was a modestly sophisticated Victorian gentlewoman and very proud of her family and social position. And like so many Victorian writers who sought to express the wisdom of their hard-earned views of life, she was alive with complexities and paradoxes. She was intensely religious, a searcher after spiritual direction and consolation, even as she was shrewdly secular, matter of fact, and down to earth. She was wilful in her passions yet eager to provide multiple and self-justifying perspectives in describing herself. She aspired to high-minded values, and she was a lover of the rude and the satiric, a woman who could at times scarcely contain the mirth that welled up within her when she witnessed an act of comedic excess or vulgarity. She was both a conservative and a progressive. She was a sharp critic of slavery and prejudice, but when moved by anger, she did not hesitate to indulge in racial stereotyping and the antisemitism typical of her era. She was a capable, independent-minded woman who married for love and became a committed wife and mother — so much so that the revelation of her sustaining and affectionate relationship with her husband provided by her surviving letters has been a surprising (even a disappointing) recognition for many readers and critics of *Roughing It in the Bush*. She was a lover of the rural, a wild country girl, yet a would-be literary woman who valued cultural distinction and achievements. She was a believer in the merits of the English class system and its traditional institutions, yet she realized that education and the liberation of the capable among the lower classes comprised the enlightened way of the future, especially in the New World.

This brief biography takes as its goal a recognition of these essential paradoxes in the life and writing of Susanna Moodie. They were part of her cultural baggage, of course, but they were part of the cultural baggage that so many British immigrants — be they English, Scottish, Irish, or Welsh — brought to British North America. In Robertson Davies' phrase, these were values and outlooks that were "bred in the bone" of the colony/country. As such, they constitute an important and distinctive legacy that Canadians neglect at their peril. Until the Second World War, English Canada largely remained a British colony in fact and in spirit; it was a vulnerable political entity of limited power, suspended by its past and its geography between the legacy inherent in its British roots and the immediacy of America's blandishments and influence.

What makes Susanna Moodie worth such attention? She stands out among the bluestockings of 1830s London — the Mary Howitts, Jane Porters, L.E.L.s, and Sarah Bowdiches, even the Agnes Stricklands — because she was deeply tested by the experience of colonial disruption. As more attention is given to these overlooked female writers, Moodie's international stock should rise considerably. Among gentlewomen writing in colonial and backwoods Upper Canada, there is no one to rival her. Anne Langton's attractive book, *A Gentlewoman in Upper Canada* (1950) came later, as did the posthumous letters of Frances Stewart (*Our Forest Home*, published privately in 1889). And while Anna Jameson saw much more of the country, given her venturesomeness and privileged position, she knew little about the harrowing struggle simply to survive year by year in the bush. Only Susanna's sister Catharine Parr Traill wrote for publication about being a pioneer and settler, and she tried her best to put a positive and cheerful interpretation on her experiences. By contrast, Moodie was interested in recording the psychological and emotional costs of her pioneering adventures; indeed, she set out to amplify and challenge her sister's account by emphasizing the kind of "misfortune" they both had come to know by 1838. So vivid is her account that it outstrips in its intensely personal power Caroline Kirkland's celebrated American record, *A New Home — Who'll Follow?* (1840), a book that, like Traill's *The Backwoods of Canada* (1836), may have served Moodie as a model.

One of Moodie's strengths as a writer is her ability to make current readers know and feel what it was like to live in Canada between the 1830s and 1850s. She takes the reader back to a time when to write about the need for change in and improvements to conditions in the colony was not only a challenge of information and perspective to the writer; it was also to be attacked and disparaged for one's lack of loyalty and to be accused of harbouring republican principles.

In writing about Susanna Moodie, both Margaret Atwood and Carol Shields have recognized her complex or split nature as a person and a writer. Atwood has envisioned her as "divided down the middle" and thus representative of the country as a whole — a country that suffers from a national illness she playfully labels "paranoid schizophrenia" (62). Writing of Moodie's published novels such as *Mark Hurdlestone; or, The Gold Worshipper* (1853), Shields conjectures that "Mrs. Moodie is unconscious of the contradictory natures of some of her characters" (19). This is to imply that the paradoxes at work in Moodie's personal vision were so deep and powerful that they escaped her own awareness. My inclination is to take Shields's observation somewhat further, to argue that Moodie herself was torn — without necessarily realizing it — between contrasting values and possibilities. Thus, in Atwood's symbolic leap, she stands as one who incarnates many important contradictions that were part of the cultural baggage brought by immigrants to Canada or that were inherent in a critical response to the difficult conditions that characterized the founding of a new (British) nation in North American space.

Part of the problem in examining Moodie's life is the need to understand the basis for and the nature of her assumptions and enthusiasms. In certain of her views, Moodie seems temptingly contemporary and thus a challenge to be understood in such terms. Moreover, the tendency to see her symbolically has proved difficult to resist, especially for those who, like Atwood, are attracted to her outspokenness and vitality and committed to demonstrating and articulating a tradition for writing that could serve post-1960s Canada.

Yet the closer one looks, the more quintessentially Victorian and colonial Moodie appears. Displaced as she was, she was still very much a woman of her time. It is worthwhile, therefore, to bring the various threads of Susanna Moodie's literary experience together so that it can be examined and assessed by those interested in her specific and general contributions. The aim of this concise biography is to bring together the important components of that record for the contemporary reader.

Moodie was above all a woman of impulsive, sometimes unyielding, emotional response, and it is precisely her strong, often opinionated responses to her experiences that have made her the central figure she has become in twentieth-century Canadian letters. It was the depth of her emotional responses and the vividness of her "lively imagination" that led her sister Catharine to apply the term "genius" to her in a retrospective profile (*Forest* 47, 49). Moodie would often say in her autobiographical writing something to this effect: 'I'm sorry if I let my feelings get the better of my argument here, but that is the way I am. You must, dear reader, TAKE ME AS I AM.' She realized that she was often led by her emotions; the truth was that, though she might apologize for her excesses, she valued her emotions above all else. While she could be convincingly rational and logical, what mattered for her was the truth of intuition, be it in the form of a gut emotional reaction, the tapping of sensibility, a commitment to deep religious feeling, or a belief in what we now call ESP. It was this inclination that made her, however briefly, a convert to Spiritualism. She explained such leanings in terms of her gender, and she strongly believed in their authority and voice.

If contradictions were involved, she could dismiss the fuss about consistency as a too-narrow, too-rational, too-constricting approach to experience. Unlike her American contemporary Walt Whitman, however, she would never have tried to raise contradiction to the level of a personal and national virtue, nor — and this may seem odd to some — could she see herself as a supporter of the transcendentalism that had fired Whitman's imagination (*Susanna Moodie* 144). Rather, she was inclined — unphilosophically, and with her religious guard relaxed — to regard variety and randomness as the stuff of life. She was certainly drawn to the comedic elements and the oddities in people she encountered. The word she most often used to describe her sketches was "droll"; it conveys her fascination with the humorously unusual, the charmingly amusing, the prankish and clownish. Had she forced herself to come to grips with what her inclinations amounted to, she might have been willing to admit, grudgingly I suspect, that what most fascinated her was the variousness, the multiplicity, the blend of seriousness and drollery she perceived within herself.

CHAPTER I

# *The English Years, 1803–32*

## STOWE HOUSE, NORWICH, AND REYDON HALL

Born on 6 December 1803 at Bungay, Suffolk, Susanna Strickland was a considerable handful from the outset. The sixth of six daughters born to Thomas and Elizabeth (Homer) Strickland, she was much petted and admired by her sisters, because of the delicacy of her health (she was baptised shortly after her birth for fear that she might soon die) and a temperament that, as it quickly came to express itself, alternately charmed and exasperated those around her. As her sister Catharine Parr fondly recalled, she was an unusual and precocious child:

> Susie was one of those eccentric children that are little understood, and being a little wild and original in her ways was often in trouble. She was either full of spirits or easily depressed, often seeing things through an excited imagination. As a very young girl she was often unhappy. It is the common fate of genius to see things through an unreal medium, either too great or too small. (*Forest* 48)

Susanna's romantic and mercurial temperament remained Catharine's strongest impression of her in later years. It was to her the mark of her sister's specialness and "genius," and, as she well knew, it continued to characterize Susanna's behaviour as a woman and a writer, though in more muted manifestations, throughout her life. Those alternations — ranging from spirited elation and delight to lonely sulkings born of unhappiness and alienation — characterize not only the important events of her life but also the autobiographical accounts of her experiences, for which she is most valued today. As she told Richard Bentley in 1854, "There is something in my character which always leads me to extremes" (*Susanna Moodie* 151).

The world Susanna Strickland entered in 1803 was initially an unsettled and perhaps unsettling one for a sickly child. Her father had only recently retired from his London position as the manager of the Greenland Dock at Rotherhithe on the Thames and had moved his family to the rural quiet and sea-air climate of the Norfolk-Suffolk border country. In family accounts, the change of scene is explained either as Thomas Strickland's search for a healthier environment (he was, according to Catharine, already crippled by gout before the move) or as his necessary adjustment in the face of discomforting financial problems he was facing in London. Whatever the case, he set up a home and office in the city of Norwich and began to look for a congenial and appropriate rural house in which he could raise and educate his daughters. Renting first near Bungay (where Susanna was born), he then leased Stowe House, a manor farm on the Flixton Road (again near Bungay), where the family lived from 1804 to 1808. A beautiful country property set above the meandering Waveney River, Stowe House was much loved by the Strickland girls, in particular by Catharine, who felt impelled to memorialize that house and the early years of the sisters in several (mostly unpublished) sketches of her childhood. They are part of the Traill Family Papers in the National Archives of Canada.

The house that seems to have stirred Susanna's fertile imagination most was Reydon Hall or Reydon House, an Elizabethan manor house two miles from the picturesque coastal town of Southwold, Suffolk. Thomas Strickland bought the property in 1808 for some three thousand pounds, removing his family from the Bungay area to its relative rural isolation. Reydon Hall was huge, drafty, and in disrepair, but its large grounds and its attics and cellars gave the younger children ample scope for their imaginative play both in and out of doors. Stories of Reydon ghosts and skulking North Sea smugglers heard from the lips of longtime servants and tenant families added to the romantic excitement of their new environment.

Here, as at Stowe House, Thomas and Elizabeth sought to educate the six girls — along with the two infant sons born at Stowe House — in academic, practical, and domestic matters. The parents stressed a curriculum of mathematics and geography as much as sewing and handicrafts, and Thomas insisted that each child take personal responsibility for his or her own garden and the care of special pets. Although his availability to oversee their academic studies was often limited because of his health and the demands of his interests in Norwich, he seems to have succeeded in inculcating in his daughters a strong sense of self-reliance, self-discipline, industry, and honesty. The capabilities that were to distinguish both Susanna and Catharine as bush settlers in Canada had their roots in his commitment to personal discipline and his love of nature.

Both Susanna and Catharine nurtured powerful memories of their father. His death, which occurred when they were impressionable teenagers, unsettled their lives and left a void that was not easily filled. Writing of him thirty years later in a piece of autobiographical fiction entitled "Rachel Wilde; or, Trifles from the Burthen of a Life," Susanna described him as "a man of great scientific and literary acquirements" and "a vigorous and independent thinker" who "acted from conscience" and "paid little regard to the received prejudices and opinions of the world." He was "a good and just man" to family, friends, and tenants, "and his family regarded him with a reverence only one degree less than that which they owed to their Creator." As she tellingly noted, "The memory of such a parent never dies; it lives for ever in the heart of his children" (*Voyages* 99). That Susanna patterned her own independent mind to a large extent on her memory of him will be evident to those who compare her moral admonitions in books such as *Roughing It in the Bush* and *Life in the Clearings versus the Bush* to her recollections of her father.

For all of his stellar qualities, however, Thomas Strickland could not in the end manage his financial resources quite as he had planned. Indeed, when he died in May 1818, he left his family in a somewhat precarious financial and social position from which the daughters had little opportunity — short of a marriage based on love (rather than on money) — to escape. While his will allowed his wife to retain possession of Reydon Hall and its tenanted lands, she had few expendable assets and little capital available to her. Financial reversals in Thomas's Norwich business, which may in fact have hastened his death, undermined his plans for his family's future. Accordingly, Strickland family life soon resolved itself in a proud struggle to keep up appearances, even as pennies had to be very carefully apportioned among the family. Mrs. Strickland managed temporarily to keep the Norwich house so that the boys could attend Dr. Valpy's school in the city, while she and the girls moved between the two houses as circumstances allowed and required.

By the mid-1820s, life at Reydon Hall had attained a resilient though static and circumscribed quality. By then, the eldest daughter, Elizabeth (Eliza, born in 1794), who had

Reydon Hall, 1980.

COURTESY ELIZABETH HOPKINS.

helped to oversee the family before and after her father's death, had left for London to pursue a career in editing and publishing. Meanwhile, the two boys were embarking upon the world at large: in 1825, Samuel (born in 1805) left to live with old family friends, the Blacks, near Darlington (now Bowmanville) in Upper Canada and to learn the skills of a settler; Thomas (born in 1807) became a sailor (and later a captain) in the employ of the East India Company. The five remaining sisters settled into the quiet life of Reydon Hall, bravely envisioning a future for themselves even as they matter-of-factly accepted the limitations that were their daily, though private, reality. Certainly, there would be no dowry to encourage marital prospects.

The social position of the Stricklands implied a comfortable leisure, and thus the outward lives of the girls were pitched to convey an appearance of well-being and gentility. Extended trips to London to visit relatives were undertaken upon invitation or when literary opportunities beckoned, but limited finances made such ventures both precious and infrequent. Agnes (born in 1796), the most advanced of the sisters as a writer, was also the most adventurous in such travel. As the decade unfolded, both Susanna and Catharine also began to taste and enjoy the opportunities of London when chances allowed. In a memoir entitled *East Anglia* (1883), James Ewing Ritchie, a young friend of Susanna, provides a valuable glimpse of Reydon Hall as he remembered it from visits in the late 1820s:

> The Stricklands had, I fancy, seen better days, and were none the worse for that . . . and the widow and the daughters kept up what little state they could; and I well remember the feeling of surprise with which I first entered their capacious drawing-room. . . . It must have been . . . a dismal old house, suggestive of rats

and dampness and mould, that Reydon Hall, with its
scantily furnished rooms and its unused attics and
its empty barns and stables, with a general air of decay
all over the place, inside and out. . . . It must have been
a difficulty with the family to keep up the place, and
the style of living was altogether plain; yet there I
heard a good deal of literary life in London. . . . (qtd.
in *Susanna Moodie* 3-4)

It was in a climate of diligent struggle to make ends meet
and keep up appearances that five of the six Strickland sisters
became published writers. Such a result evolved naturally
from their rural isolation and the shared activities of their
childhood years — putting on plays, experimenting with
poetry (especially of flowers, local scenes, and girlhood pleasures), and, under the stimulation of the histories that they
read in their father's library, writing narratives based on the
heroic characters who most attracted them. Moreover, such
enterprise — naïve and entirely personal at first — was
among the kinds of activity in which middle-class girls could
properly engage. Catharine was the first of the sisters to be
published. In 1818, just after her father's death, a family friend
picked up by chance one of her manuscript stories while
he was visiting Reydon. So taken with it was he that he
carried it off to London, where he soon found an interested
publisher. Within a year, she was a published author and the
recipient of a small but very welcome payment for the outright
sale of her copyright. With this tangible encouragement
before the sisters, a pattern of emulation and competition at
Reydon Hall began in earnest.

Susanna Strickland's authorial propensities emerged early.
Catharine remembered that her sister quickly became "a
great reader" and, by "the age of nine or ten years," had begun
"to clothe her ideas and feelings in verse. Her facility for

rhyme was great and her imagination vivid and romantic, tinged with gloom and grandeur more than wit and humour" (*Forest* 48). By her teens, she had focused that passionate commitment upon romantic and warlike figures such as Prince Eugene of Germany and Napoleon. Her father, however, was quick to challenge her "Bonaparte mania" on the grounds that Napoleon was, among other things, "the enemy of her country." Knowing his daughter's mercurial temperament and her resistance to rebuke, he adopted a strategy that worked admirably as an educational tool, if not precisely as a means of changing her mind. Having invited her to discuss the matter, by agreement he then "entered into correspondence with her," thereby forcing her to think through her ideas and to "study" the proofs she used to justify her opinions. From her point of view, the exercise, in which she participated "with all her heart and soul," taught her "to think" and to weigh carefully her "impressions" and "reflections" (*Voyages* 141) before she sought to include them in her narratives.

While a young teenager, Susanna began to write her "early productions." Catharine recalled the many "very pleasant times" they shared "reading, writing and taking long walks" together in the solitude of the Reydon Hall grounds (*Forest* 52). Although Susanna nurtured the notion of herself as "a solitary child" and a wayward spirit who was often and unfairly made "the general scape-goat" of her sisters (*Voyages* 138, 150), it is clear that she had a special bond with Catharine, in both their shared bouts of writing and their emotional affinity. "The strong affection that this dear sister always felt for me," Catharine recalled, "had great power in toning down the troubled spirit" (*Forest* 49). Susanna later cast Catharine as her beloved Dorothea in her autobiographical narrative "Rachel Wilde." Rachel, she wrote, "loved this kind sister" who "had a perfect controll [sic] over her passions" and was her "one faithful friend and counselor."

Her "affection for her . . . fell little short of idolatry"; indeed, though Rachel was often "untractable to others, she was tractable to Dorothea" (*Voyages* 137). That intractableness, often a source of conflict with her older sisters, was particularly directed at Eliza, to whom "she was no favourite" (*Voyages* 149). (Susanna's often rocky relationship with Agnes is more fully detailed in this study.)

The young Susanna was impelled to write in several modes. Beyond the narratives for children that became a kind of family staple in the 1820s, she wrote poetry and tragedies in the mode of "gloom and grandeur" (*Voyages* 48) that to Catharine was characteristic of her early effusions. Tragedies had a great appeal to Susanna, and works such as "Henrie," "The Bride of Brittany," and "Bourbon" were among her "first attempts at authorship"; when she was in her twenties, however, she was convinced to burn them by "foolish fanaticks, with whom I got entangled," who regarded the theatre and acting as activities "unworthy of a christian" (*Susanna Moodie* 164).

In her teenage years, Susanna was often unhappy, at war with governesses or certain of her sisters and "constantly brooding" on themes of grandeur and mystery (*Voyages* 138-39). Catharine recalled one occasion, likely in 1816, when the older and very businesslike Eliza suddenly returned to Reydon from Norwich. Finding Catharine and Susanna beguiling the tedium of a long winter by writing novels, Eliza coldly dismissed such work as trash and their efforts as a waste of time. Susanna's reaction might well have been predicted; indignantly, she threw her manuscript into the fire and retired to her room in inconsolable distress and anger. In retelling the story in "Rachel Wilde," she re-creates the overwhelming sense of unfairness and cruelty that she, the "hapless author," felt when Eliza (cast as Lilla) belittled her "sacred Manuscript." Calling her a "chit," Lilla dismissed the indulgent "nonsense" as fit only to serve as a covering for the pig then roasting on the fire (*Voyages* 149-50). That memory remained for Susanna like a live charcoal in her consciousness thirty years later.

## LITERARY FRIENDS AND
## LONDON LITERARY MARKETS

It was the emergence of new opportunities for writing in London that provided a start for Agnes, Jane Margaret (born in 1800), Catharine (born in 1802), and Susanna as published writers. Only Sarah (born in 1798) was not interested in writing. Two markets opened simultaneously for the Strickland girls. The first was the growing interest of small-scale publishers in short readable stories for children and adolescents. The subjects could vary from historical narrative to adventure to scenes of daily life, but the substance had to confirm the importance of firm moral principle, obedience to one's elders, and exemplary Christian behaviour. Working in a tradition characterized by books such as Thomas Day's *Sandford and Merton* (1783-89), Sarah Trimmer's *Fabulous Histories* (1786), Maria Edgeworth's *Moral Tales* (1801), and Charles and Mary Lamb's *Mrs. Leicester's School* (1809), Susanna Strickland was first published in 1822 by A.K. Newman, who had long since taken over the Minerva Press in London from William Lane. *Spartacus: A Roman Story* was the first and longest of a series of narratives and long poems she wrote about legendary historical heroes who fascinated her, among them Gustavus Adolphus, Arminius, and William Wallace. The book, she recalled, was taken to London by a family friend, James Black, who arranged for its publication and brought back ten pounds for its delighted and surprised author (*Susanna Moodie* 216).

Susanna in fact congratulated herself on rescuing Spartacus from "the oblivion with which Roman historians have
laboured to cover his name" (*Spartacus* 61). But while she
gloried in reclaiming such a hero — a man who had become
a great warrior against his will and who was in her terms a
being "almost above humanity" (11) — she faced the problem
of constructing a plot that would confirm his stature as a
nobly motivated rebel without sullying his stature as a good
man. Her solution was to locate the blame for the rebellion
in a barbarian named Theodoric, whose lust for battle draws
the peace-loving, high-minded Spartacus to his ennobling
death. While the book is a serious-minded and passionate
tribute to its hero, it is also an overwritten and naïve celebration of Spartacus's nobility and sensibility. As a hero, he
can do no wrong; accordingly, his martyrdom is exemplary.

Writing to provide moral guidance for youthful readers in
an entertaining and dramatic form, Susanna Strickland, like
her sisters, had considerable success in finding supportive
publishers over the next decade. Her primary publisher at the
outset was Dean and Munday. That firm seems to have
shared many of its titles with the aforementioned publisher
and bookseller, A.K. Newman. Led by its enterprising female
partners, Mary Ann Dean (a master printer since 1814) and
Anna Maria Munday, Dean and Munday became one of the
most active and innovative among publishers of illustrated
children's books in the early years of the century. It seems
gradually to have taken the lead in negotiations and publishing from Newman. The firm (which later became Thomas
Dean and Co. and still later Dean and Sons) continued to
reprint books by Susanna and Catharine long after both
had emigrated to Canada. As the years went by, its staff
occasionally confused the authorship of various titles by
the Strickland sisters; for example, it attributed to Susanna
Catharine's *Little Downy: or, The History of a Field Mouse*, a

story first published in 1822 (its author was originally identified only as Miss Black) and one that, according to Elizabeth Strickland, was still very popular in London stores in the 1860s.

Although the publishing details provided by such firms remain problematic today (especially with regard to authorship and dating), it is clear that Susanna's tales for children during the 1820s and early 1830s included *The Little Quaker; or, Josiah Shirley* (also published with the subtitle *The Triumph of Virtue*), *The Sailor Brother; or, The History of Thomas Saville*, *The Little Prisoner; or, Passion and Patience* (1829), *Hugh Latimer; or, The School-Boy's Friendship* (a copy of which bears the date 1828 on its frontispiece), *Rowland Massingham: or, I Will Be My Own Master*, and *Profession and Principle; or, The Vicar's Tales*. Susanna also told Richard Bentley that her little book *Mamma's Fairy Tales in Rhyme* was published by Samuel Maunder, "who was always a kind friend" during these years. Several of these little books sold well, she recalled, and Hugh Latimer (to which she wrote a sequel) went through "many editions" (*Susanna Moodie* 216).

Interestingly, Susanna's conduct books were almost exclusively about young boys. She often poised her narrative upon a contrast of types. The one in need of reform and self-control is well born, arrogant, selfish, and insensitive to the feelings of others — a forerunner to that most wilful of Victorian youths, Charles Dickens's Steerforth. For all his charm and good manners, he is initially blind to the humanity of those below his class. His social and heroic opposite is humbly born, generous, and sometimes easily led, but at heart noble of spirit. In the plot, the aristocratic youth takes advantage of his superior position to discredit or humiliate his opposite, but in the end (and in such plots the end can sometimes seem a long way off), a powerful nemesis prevails. The privileged boy is made to recognize his cruelty and folly in ways that are at times painful but always instructive. In *The Little Prisoner*, for instance, Ferdinand is given a taste of incarceration by his stern but wise father, while in *Rowland Massingham* (the subtitle of which defines young Rowland's problem), the aristocratic protagonist maims his left hand while playing with a forbidden gun. In those cases where the contrast applies, the humble boy's fine qualities of character are finally recognized for what they are and duly rewarded.

Such simplistic "English" plots, clothed in more engaging detail and applying a variety of narrative devices, remained Susanna Strickland's staple as a fiction writer throughout her life. They are as evident in *Geoffrey Moncton; or, The Faithless Guardian* (1855) as in *Hugh Latimer*, which appears to have been published in 1828. Taken together, they indicate the extent to which Susanna was rooted in a cultural plot she could not imaginatively escape for long. That plot required, within the dictates and perimeters of an aristocratic, class-conscious, and materialistic society, the recognition of her protagonist's — and her own — value as an individual fully deserving of elevation and reward within the social order in which he or she had been misplaced.

Strong social fables thus underlie these narratives. Much as Susanna Strickland identified romantically with noble rebel figures such as Spartacus, she was governed in her narratives by a faith in a benevolent and noble paternalism (usually in the form of fathers, guardians, or ministers) that would eventually recognize the worth and correct the fortunes of her humbly born protagonist. Such narratives are romances of rectified order in which merit, commitment to education, and the enactment of principled moral behaviour provide the keys to a long-delayed social adjustment. At their most optimistic and romantic, they provide an apotheosis of the kind orchestrated by a fairy godmother. In the pious tone characteristic of these stories, the uncle of the orphaned

Hugh Latimer provides the definitive blueprint for good behaviour:

> But, Hugh Latimer, if you pursue virtue, and stead-
> fastly adhere to the paths of truth, even if you were
> a beggar's brat, you would, by this course, gain the
> esteem of the good and sensible part of mankind, and
> need not fear the ridicule of those who wantonly com-
> mit crime, because they think that their rank shields
> them. (*Hugh Latimer* 9-10)

The ethic of such narratives is explicitly Christian and conservative; it is also implicitly romantic and materialistic.
Hugh overcomes his envy of social position and proves himself a meritorious individual. He never ceases, however, to
feel "that proper diffidence which ought to be paid to those
of superior rank" (120); neither is he blind to the ways in
which rank and riches provide a lustre to moral worth,
whatever its source. He learns to excuse "early prejudices"
bred by "the outside show of titles" (134-35). What matters
is inner virtue, which is the true source of goodness and the
basis for a proper recognition of one's real value and social
merit.

While these early narratives focus on male protagonists
and guides, it is clear that the distinctive pattern of rescue
they enact owes something to the Cinderella myth, a story
of great pertinence to the longings for recognition and improved social rank among middle-class members of England's
aristocratic order. At heart, Susanna Strickland was no doubt
disappointed in and frustrated by the limitations of her social
position in rural Suffolk, fatherless, dowryless, and relatively
penniless as she was. Romantically, however, she could imagine the possibilities of rescue and elevation, and, within
the requirements of a socially conservative form of popular

fiction for children, she could plot the satisfyingly improved fates of her long-suffering, mistreated, but noble protagonists.

The second market Susanna discovered was the world of gift-book annuals that became popular in the early 1820s. Ushered in by a German-born London publisher named Rudolph Ackermann and his literary editor, Frederic Shoberl, these Christmas and New Year's anthologies of poems, sketches, and stories — packaged with attractive sentimental engravings related to poignant aspects of the literary material — were soon a seasonal craze among middle-class consumers. As the decade wore on, competition between publishers for well-known editors, contributors, and engravers became fierce, and literary periodicals such as the *Athenaeum* and the *Literary Gazette* reviewed and puffed the many volumes vying for popular attention. While Susanna did manage to have a few of her poems published as early as 1825, she was soon placing her poetry and stories with several of the annuals. Indeed, in 1830 she proudly reported to Thomas Pringle, then the editor of *Friendship's Offering*, that her work would appear in seven annuals that year; in addition to Pringle's annual, she would be in the *Amulet, Ackermann's Juvenile Forget-Me-Not*, the *Iris*, the *New Year's Gift*, the *Juvenile Keepsake*, and *Emmanuel*, sometimes under experimental pseudonyms.

As a fledgling writer seeking the wider literary exposure and recognition already achieved by her older sister Agnes, who had made several appearances in Colburn's *New Monthly Magazine* and had two collections of her poems published in the 1820s, Susanna found her big opportunity through an old Suffolk family friend, Thomas Harral, who had taken over a London magazine called the *Belle Assemblée*, devoted to fashion and literature. Harral's daughter Laura, herself an occasional contributor to the magazine, was a close friend of Susanna's, while Laura's brother, Francis, was engaged for a time to Susanna's sister Catharine. From April 1827 until 1831, when Harral lost the magazine, Susanna contributed poems and sketches, over fifty pieces in all, and gained increasing attention as a promising writer among the young bluestockings of the day.

In retrospect, the most important of her *Belle Assemblée* contributions were her five Suffolk sketches (1827-29), in particular "Old Hannah: or, The Charm" (1829). Here, for the first time, and with evident success, Susanna adopted an attractively personal, first-person narrative voice and, with freshness of effect, contrasted her own buoyant and youthful interest in life with the superstitiousness and sentimental expectations of the elderly Hannah, a crusty Reydon Hall servant of long experience and little education other than in the folk ways of her native county. While Susanna's brothers play a thoughtless practical joke that takes advantage of Hannah's still lively marital hopes, the narrator remains fascinated by the "inscrutable" knowledge that Hannah imparts to her (*Voyages* 17). "Hannah first initiated me in ghostly lore," as well as gypsies, cures, and charms; such information the young narrator "infinitely preferred to the detested task of conning my lessons" (16).

What emerges from the sketch is the narrator's own fascination with spiritualism, magic, and romantic love. Passing no judgement on Hannah's views and actions (that is left to her "roguish" and "mischievous" brothers [*Voyages* 20, 24]), the narrator is nevertheless so affected by the absurdity of Hannah's midnight terror that she "was constrained to turn my back on the afflicted damsel, to hide the painful risibility with which I was irresistibly assailed" (21). Her sense of the absurd does not, however, lead her to dismiss Hannah's beliefs. She remains fascinated by matters largely closed to rational inquiry and by a strength of mind utterly resistant to what is readily explicable. Although Susanna occasionally returned to this narrative approach in the years before her emigration, it was not one she seems initially to have favoured. It would, however, serve her very well in her three autobiographical Canadian books. Indeed, first-person representation proved to be the key to her most enduring work as a professional writer.

As Susanna Strickland became better known as a writer of promise, she developed a number of literary connections and came to enjoy some of the flavour and the blandishments of London literary society. Each of her literary links tells us something about the important forces and interests that fed her development as a writer. Each opens a door to a certain aspect of her thinking and a potential she would develop — in one way or another — in her later Canadian work. At the same time, these connections make it clear that, when the adventure — for adventure it surely was — of being recognized and celebrated as a promising English writer gave way to the new adventure of marriage, parenthood, and emigration, she faced a loss she had difficulty accepting at first. It was a loss she sublimated as best she could.

Beyond Thomas Harral, who was the author of many historical books and a figure of great accomplishment to Susanna, she and her sisters became intimates with Harral's valued friend, the agreeable and kindly James Bird, and his wife, Emma. Bird, known fondly in Suffolk as the bard of Yoxford, lived in the quiet village of that name about ten miles from Reydon. His long poems about famous historical locales in Suffolk — for example, *Dunwich; A Tale of the Splendid City* (1828) and *Framlingham: A Narrative of the Castle* (1831) — were among the Strickland girls' favourites. His writing had earned him a local fame and a London reputation in which the sisters were eager to bask. They made his home and bookshop-cum-drugstore a stopping point whenever they could manage a means of conveyance from

Reydon to Yoxford. Susanna, a particular favourite with the
Birds and their children (she was godmother to their son
Walter), learned from James much about the study and celebration of the local. Through his poetry and conversation,
she expanded her love of East Anglian antiquity and her
delight in the simple life of the country. Her aforementioned
Suffolk sketches and many of her poems owe much to the
model he provided, while her letters to him suggest the range
not only of playfulness but also of religious seriousness that
their friendship encompassed.

A second set of local connections relate to Susanna Strickland's fast-developing personal commitment to religion. As a
family, the Stricklands were confirmed Anglicans, especially
after the death of the father, and it was as an Anglican
that Susanna was "suddenly awakened" in her twenties. Her
arousal from a state of "doubtful questioning" and "indiffer-
ence" to one of intense inquiry and searching occurred when
she came under the influence of "an enthusiastic clergyman
of the English Church" in Southwold (*Forest* 50). In Catharine's recollection, that churchman, thinking more about
the requirements of spiritual guidance than of denomination,
directed Susanna to "the care of a worthy earnest Nonconformist Pastor" named James Ritchie when he himself
was removed from the area (51). Ritchie was the minister of
the Congregationalist Church of Wrentham, a village near
Reydon. Susanna spent considerable time with the Ritchie
family, absorbing the doctrine of their church and studying
flower painting under the tutelage of Ritchie's wife. By means
of his guidance and against the strong objections of her
mother and sisters Agnes and Jane, Susanna prepared herself
for acceptance into the Congregational Church and took the
precipitous step of personal conversion in April 1830 (see
*Susanna Moodie* 43-48). Although soon she would again alter
her religious course to meet her changing emotional needs,

the influence of the Ritchies would stay with her throughout her lifetime. Her skill as a still-life painter, which she passed on to her daughter Agnes, would prove a modest source of income in Canada, while her religious questing would continue through a variety of incarnations in her adopted country.

Susanna's conversion to James Ritchie's nonconformist church is less surprising than it might appear. Those were days of indulgence and stultification in the Anglican Church, an era of "fox-hunting, horse-riding men in our Suffolk churches." It was a "truly Gospel sermon" in Reydon parish church — the first such preaching she had heard in years — that aroused Susanna, and she was, it would seem, never the same again. The real vitality of religious expression in northeastern Suffolk (with the notable exception of the aforementioned Southwold clergyman) lay at this time in its nonconformist churches and in a more personal and passionate kind of expression than was found in Anglican ritual "under the reign of the Georges" (*Forest* 51).

In fact, there seems to have been considerable social interaction between members of different Suffolk denominations at this time. For instance, on the basis of an independent-minded, intellectual friendship between Thomas Strickland and John Childs, the Stricklands had become family acquaintances of the Childses of Bungay, likely before they moved to Reydon. The Childses were prominent Methodists and political radicals who ran a flourishing publishing business, producing cheap Bibles and inexpensive series of "Standard Authors" while challenging the Bible-printing monopoly sanctioned by the English government. True to his beliefs, John Childs (1783-1853) carried on a long dispute against the unfairness of such patronage and went to jail in 1835 for refusing to pay the church rates imposed on all nonconformists by church and state. His actions earned him political and religious notoriety as "the Bungay martyr." Susanna

Strickland and her sisters certainly spent time visiting the
Childses. There they met prominent local intellectuals and
nonconformists and took part in debates about the issues of
the day. There too they imbibed the gospel of phrenology,
an interest shared by both John and his eccentric brother
Robert.

Now regarded as a pseudoscience, phrenology was a naïve
form of psychology so much the rage during the 1820s and 1830s
that it left a distinctive mark on much Victorian writing. One
finds its traces virtually everywhere in the observations of the
Strickland sisters. Based on their mapping of the contours
and shape of the skull, phrenologists believed that they could
use the outer to explain the inner, that the bumps and valleys
on an individual's head provided the keys to character and
behaviour. With the inadvertent loss of much of her hair and
some of her considerable dignity, Agnes Strickland reputedly
allowed Robert Childs to make a bust of her head for his
skull museum. Both Susanna and Catharine would remember Robert's phrenological passion in stories about what
they jokingly called his "Scullery" or "Golgotha." Susanna's
"Washing the Black-a-Moor White" can be found in *Voyages*
(253-56). Catharine's story "Cousin Kate: or the Professor
Outwitted" (*Forest* 31-45), plays, among other things, with
the long-standing engagement between her sister Sarah, the
beauty of the Strickland family, and Robert Childs. When
Sarah and Robert finally married in 1835, Agnes and Jane,
who were staunch Anglicans, objected to the union, just as
they had resisted Susanna's dramatic conversion to Congregationalism. Robert apparently committed suicide about
1838, and the Childs family made little effort to provide
financial help to Sarah in her widowhood. Perhaps not surprisingly, in her *Life of Agnes Strickland* (1887), Jane Margaret
Strickland elected to erase the Strickland-Childs marriage
from the record, making much instead of Sarah's second

marriage to Canon Richard Gwillym, an Anglican minister. Jane treated it as if it had been Sarah's first. The record thus falsely presents the Stricklands as devotedly Anglican. Nowhere, of course, is Susanna's Congregational experience mentioned.

Nonconformism was an outlook that Susanna Strickland embraced in 1829-30 with all the force of her romantic enthusiasm. The word *enthusiasm* is in fact one she deliberately chose to align herself with, for "enthusiasm" — literally, a recognition and celebration of God within — was a verbal sign of faith of a deeply emotional and special kind, a faith that extended to include a love of nature (be it benign or demonic) and a poetic awe before the illimitable range of God's handiwork. Enthusiasm was an idea with a long and controversial history, and, as Susan Glickman has ably argued, it had been much sullied by the eighteenth-century rationalists. In his dictionary, for instance, Samuel Johnson defined it variously as "a vain belief of private revelation; a vain confidence of divine favour or communication," as well as "[h]eat of imagination" and "elevation of fancy" (qtd. in Glickman 15). For Susanna, however, enthusiasm was a blessed and elevated state of consciousness, of spiritual and imaginative perception that she linked directly to divine inspiration. Not surprisingly, she wrote a long poem by that title and chose it as the title poem of her ambitious 1831 collection, *Enthusiasm, and Other Poems*. Although marketed by Smith and Elder in London, it was organized in part by her Congregational pastor, James Ritchie, and was printed and sold by subscription by John Childs in Bungay.

While the idea of enthusiasm had a strong appeal to Susanna, her religious commitment was, for all its fervour, restless and evolving. It involved many shifts and passages. Awakening to religious awareness as an Anglican, she became deeply interested in biblical texts, especially Old

Testament visions of annihilation and apocalypse. In this spirit in February and March 1829, she contributed biblical paraphrases and other poems ("The Vision of Dry Bones," "By Babel's Stream," "The Burden of Babylon," and "Elijah in the Wilderness") to the *Ecclesiastic: A Religious and Family Paper*, a short-lived London magazine with something of an antislavery bent. Thomas Pringle and Jane Margaret Strickland were other contributors. Her letters of the period also mention a religious project initiated by Robert Childs — "a small volume of Psalms and Hymns as an accompaniment to the Hora Religiones" (*Susanna Moodie* 29) — that suggests her interest in making a literary contribution of a nondenominational kind.

*Enthusiasm, and Other Poems* was an expression of the dedication of her "soul and song" to God. In the high-toned cadences of the title poem, Susanna sought to define the idea as she had experienced it:

> Parent of genius, bright Enthusiasm!
> Bold nurse of high resolve and generous thought,
> 'Tis to thy soul-awakening power we owe
> The preacher's eloquence, the painter's skill,
> The poet's lay, the patriot's noble zeal,
> The warrior's courage, and the sage's lore.
> Oh! till the soul is quickened by thy breath,
> Wit, wisdom, eloquence, and beauty, fail
> To make a just impression on the heart;
> The tide of life creeps lazily along,
> Soiled with the stains of earth, and man debased
> Sinks far below the level of the stream. (2-3)

Awakened herself from the lazy "tide of life" that had previously bemused and constrained her, she felt herself energized and focused in a powerful and enabling way. What enthusiasm gave her was the artistic licence to follow her romantic propensities, certain that, so long as her resolve was "high" and her thought "generous," the poet in her would align itself with the preacher, the patriot, the painter, the sage, and the warrior. The list itself is indicative, for Susanna had something of each in her nature.

Although the volume of forty-seven poems suffered from what the *Athenaeum* of 28 May 1831 called youthfully "careless versification," its shorter poems, which the reviewer preferred, evinced "a tone of tender seriousness which marks a refined and reflective mind" (342). It begins with two long poems that in retrospect reflect Susanna Strickland's characteristic ambivalence during this period. While "Enthusiasm" concerns itself with inspiration that lifts the soul "above its sensual, vain delights" (3), "Fame" seeks to identify the lures and penalties of a too secular approach to life. Although Susanna sought in the latter poem to reduce the pursuit of fame to a vain dream, her close attention to its dangers and distractions indicates the attraction it represented for her. Indeed, as Glickman has shown, most of the volume reflects the intensity and self-consciousness that characterized Susanna's thinking in the late 1820s (11). Her later description of these poems as the work of her adolescence is a misrepresentation of *Enthusiasm, and Other Poems*, a work that reflects the force of her multiple awakenings and her struggle as a writer to position herself for the future (*Susanna Moodie* 147).

A variant of enthusiastic passion — in Susanna's terms — animates the four poems, matched with four by Agnes, that made up *Patriotic Songs*, a small pamphlet that appeared to positive reviews a few months after *Enthusiasm, and Other Poems*. It reminds us that the passion for England and the monarchy, shared here by the two sisters, would lead Agnes to her work as the celebrated historian of England's and Scotland's queens. In her colonial setting, Susanna would take up the patriotic banner when the threat of rebellion reached Upper Canada late in 1837.

The joint undertaking must have been a curious one, for Agnes had been much vexed by Susanna's conversion to Congregationalism and had apparently ceased for a while to communicate with her sister. Catharine noted with happiness their reconciliation in 1831. Susanna's contributions, which included "The Land of Our Birth," "The Banner of England," and "God Preserve the King," earned her at least as much recognition as Agnes received from reviewers; moreover, as she recalled in a letter of 25 July 1874 to the editor of the Toronto *Globe* (see *Susanna Moodie* 315), the "joint volume" won "the two country girls" the praise of King William IV, who called them "an ornament to our country." Regrettably, no copy of *Patriotic Songs*, published in Soho (with music included by its publisher, J. Green), has survived to my knowledge. The book can only be identified by means of reviews.

The battle between the inward call of religious enthusiasm and the outward appeal of public recognition and literary achievement raged in Susanna Strickland's heart and imagination throughout these years of her awakening. Thus, even as she imagined herself retreating from the wicked, secular world toward some refuge of nunlike purity, she was eager to increase her contacts with the British literati. In the summer of 1829, for example, she succeeded in initiating a personal correspondence with Mary Russell Mitford, whom she described, fawningly but accurately, as "one of the first of our female writers" (*Susanna Moodie* 39). The author of tragedies performed in London and most famous, both then and now, as a writer of charming rural sketches about her native Berkshire area (the *Our Village* collections were published between 1824 and 1832), Mitford proved friendly and open to the young writer's overtures. In describing herself to Mitford

as both a "plain, matter-of-fact country girl" and "one of
Fancy's spoiled and wayward children, [who] from the age
of twelve years ha[s] roamed through the beautiful but delusive
regions of Romance, entirely to gratify my restless imagination" (*Susanna Moodie* 38), Susanna almost inadvertently
defined another duality of her sensibility. The realistic and
the romantic, the matter of fact and the fanciful, both had
powerful claims upon her melodramatic sensibility.

So frank were her letters that Susanna succeeded in ingra-
tiating herself to Mitford. With evident excitement, she
shared her literary aspirations and her observations on
the passing literary scene as she was discovering it. From
Mitford, whom she seems never to have met in person, she
received sensible advice about the consequences of fame and
a respectful interest in her prospects that she must have
found encouraging.

The most important of her literary connections was Thomas
Pringle (1789-1834), whom Susanna described lovingly to
Mitford in 1830 as "my dear adopted father" (*Susanna Moodie*
50). A Scot with extended literary experience in his native
land (he had helped to found *Blackwood's Magazine* in 1817),
Pringle joined a number of his fellow countrymen in emigrating to South Africa, where, prevented from farming by
a physical handicap, he edited a newspaper in Capetown.
After several years, however, his antislavery views led to the
loss of his position. Returning to London, he took up literary
work of various kinds and was appointed Secretary of the
Anti-Slavery Society in March 1827.

It may well have been through Thomas Harral that
Susanna met Pringle and his wife, Mary. She first mentions
Pringle in a letter of May 1828. By November, he was helping
her to make publishing contacts in London. She was likely a
welcome visitor in the Pringle house by 1829, and she was
certainly a special guest of the family in the summer of 1830

while the Pringles summered in the village of Hampstead.
While sojourning with them there and in London, she met
many famous London figures of the day: the painter John
Martin (whose soirées she occasionally attended and whose
apocalyptic paintings fascinated her), Leitch Ritchie,
Thomas Roscoe, and Mrs. Sara Bowdich, to name a few.

But the three most important introductions Susanna received at the Pringles' were to people less known in and
unfamiliar with the great city. The first two were Caribbean
slaves, Mary Prince and Ashton Warner. Mary, whose married name was James, was a Bermuda-born black woman who
had been a slave in Antigua and in 1830-31 was living with —
and nominally at least working for — the Pringles. Recently
celebrated by scholars as "the first black British woman to
escape from slavery and publish a record of her experiences"
(Ferguson 1), Black Mary, as Susanna fondly called her, had
such a compelling and harrowing story to tell that Thomas
Pringle arranged to have it "taken down from Mary's own
lips by a lady who happened to be at the time residing in my
family as a visitor" (Ferguson 45). That lady was Susanna
Strickland.

The resulting pamphlet, published in 1831 in London and
Edinburgh but independent of the Anti-Slavery Society,
went through three editions that year. The graphic details of
whippings and cruelty, along with the documentary evidence
of her "owner's" continuing claims upon her, helped to stir
indignation in a British populace that was increasingly at
odds with the continuing legality of the institution in British
colonies. Asserting that the greatest care had been taken by
Susanna Strickland in recording Mary's "exact expressions
and peculiar phraseology," Pringle verified the authenticity
of the facts and the substance of the "tract" in his preface
(dated 25 January 1831). At the same time, he reported that,
to make the document "clearly intelligible" and evocative,

it had been necessary that he and Susanna "prune . . . [it] into its present shape," deleting "redundances and gross grammatical errors" (Ferguson 45). The resulting document, the profits from which were to go to Mary Prince herself, was thus rendered literary by its editors and for their purposes a more effective means of persuading the public of slavery's perniciousness. Little could Susanna have imagined in 1831 that the work of hers most read around the world in the 1990s would be this small contribution to the work of the anti-slavery movement, a contribution only marginally connected to her larger literary endeavours by the editor of the 1987 reprint of Mary Prince's account.

The exercise, however, had a profound effect upon Susanna, no doubt aligning itself by its moral authority with other dimensions of her enthusiasm. While with the Pringles, her social conscience was stirred, deepened, and given voice. As she reported in her introduction to the second pamphlet (dated 19 February 1831), *Negro Slavery Described by a Negro: Being the Narrative of Ashton Warner, a Native of St. Vincent's*, she had been, "until a few months ago, one of the apathetical and deluded class I am now animadverting upon." No longer willing to be "a sharer in a great national crime," she described her conversion:

The entire change in my own ideas, in regard to slavery, was chiefly effected by the frequent opportunities which Providence recently and unexpectedly threw in my way of conversing with several negroes, both male and female, who had been British colonial slaves, and who had borne in their own persons the marks of the brand and the whip, and had drunk the bitter cup to its dregs. To their simple and affecting narrative I could not listen unmoved. The voice of truth and nature prevailed over my former prejudices. I beheld slavery unfolded in its revolting details; and, having been thus irresistibly led to peruse the authentic accounts of the real character and effects of the system, I am resolved no longer to be an accomplice to its criminality, though it were only by keeping silence regarding it. (6)

Thus aroused, Susanna served as amanuensis for Ashton Warner, a twenty-four-year-old slave who offered "striking proofs of what the African is capable, were his mental powers suffered to expand under the genial influences of civilization and Christianity." Unlike Mary Prince, however, Warner was in very poor health. By the time the "little tract" was prepared, he was suffering from a "severe illness" (12). Then, in the pamphlet's advertisement (a late addition dated 1 March 1831), it was announced that Warner had died and that any benefits from the pamphlet's sale would be directed to his "aged mother and the enfranchisement of his enslaved wife and child." That Thomas Pringle had to absorb personal financial loss for the Warner project, she learned later. Little wonder that some of Susanna's poems of this period — for example, "An Appeal to the Free!" (*Athenaeum*, 20 November 1830; see *Enthusiasm* 77-79) — addressed the question of slavery with a passionate sense of wrong and injustice:

> Ye children of Britain! brave sons of the Isles
> Who revel in freedom and bask in her smiles,
> Can ye yet sanction such deeds as are done in the West,
> And sink on your pillows untroubled to rest? (78)

Little wonder too that her hostility to complacent ideas about slavery was still much alive in certain of the social encounters she recalled in *Roughing It in the Bush* and *Flora Lyndsay: or, Passages in an Eventful Life* (1854).

## JOHN WEDDERBURN DUNBAR MOODIE

The other guest Susanna Strickland met at the Pringles had a lifelong effect upon her. While in South Africa, Pringle, whose African poems and memoir, *African Sketches* (1834), are still much valued, was friendly with Scottish brothers of Orkney lineage. Donald Moodie and his younger brother, John Wedderburn Dunbar, had emigrated with Pringle to the Cape colony to take up farming. In 1830, while Donald, who would later have a distinguished career as an administrator and writer in South Africa, remained behind, John took a long furlough to London. He had two primary goals in mind: the completion and publication of a book he had begun about his South African experiences, and the attempt to find a wife whom he might persuade to return with him to his African farm.

Unattached and lonely, they met at the Pringles in the summer of 1830. Awash in contradiction, Susanna was fresh from her conversion to Congregationalism but very excited about her current adventures in London literary society. John was a member of a once distinguished Orkney family (the family home of Melsetter on the island of Hoy had been lost to creditors by 1819), a veteran half-pay officer of the 21st Royal (Northern) Fusiliers who had been wounded during his service in the Napoleonic Wars, a traveller and adventurer, an amateur musician, and a published author with a major work in progress. At thirty-six years of age and with an eye for attractive women, he was hungry for sympathetic and spirited company. The two of them spent hours together wandering the heath at Hampstead. Within a few weeks, they had established the basis for a relationship that would sustain itself over their thirty-eight years together.

Writing to James Bird in August 1830, Susanna described herself as in "an ecstasy of fear lest my Dunbar's Regiment

Melsetter House.

REPRINTED FROM *SCOTTISH COUNTRY LIFE* (AUGUST 1980).

should be called into action" to meet the threats of the new "French Revolution" (*Susanna Moodie* 49). Herself a veteran of several romantic entanglements obliquely and incompletely referred to in family correspondence, Susanna was intense and mercurial in her feelings for John Moodie. The relationship, so suddenly compelling and serious, involved the two of them in the need to make what seemed to be inescapable and categorical decisions. If they married, as they wished to do, and if they were to maintain their established social position, they would have to plan carefully where and how they would live, and they would need financial support of some acceptable kind. As neither had immediate expectations of inheritance or even a modest source of income (except for John's military half-pension and the uncertain prospect of literary earnings), they shared the view that it would be impossible to set up a home and raise a family in Britain. John's personal plan involved South Africa, but Susanna found that prospect daunting, particularly in light of the vivid descriptions that he had written about the dangers and hairbreadth escapes he had experienced there. An aversion to large animals — elephants, tigers, and lions were particularly horrific and exotic for her — fed her fear of such a strange and different world. Caught between what seemed to be the opportunity of her life and her great fear of what South Africa represented, she urged John to seek a better alternative for them.

While John journeyed to the Orkneys later that summer to renew family connections and investigate financial opportunities, Susanna awaited his return throughout the autumn of 1830. She was, however, uneasy at Reydon Hall, preoccupied by the "curse of authorship," which "cleave[d]" to her like "the garment of Hercules," and realizing that it might be her last winter there with her mother (who had little interest in "the blue stocking fraternity") and sisters (*Susanna Moodie*

**Moodie family crest.**

FROM A REPRINT OF THE 1852 EDITION
OF *ROUGHING IT IN THE BUSH.*

52). At the same time, she was wrestling with guilt and embarrassment during her continuing visits to the Ritchies in Wrentham. Although James Ritchie was helping her to arrange for the publication of and subscription to *Enthusiasm, and Other Poems*, he was clearly displeased with his protégé's sudden engagement to a Presbyterian and a soldier. One of John's surviving letters to her (7 September-2 October 1830) alludes angrily to a letter from Ritchie that "persecut[ed]" Susanna for her change of plans and sought to interfere with them. Without questioning Ritchie's honesty and sincerity, Moodie deemed him "a man whose mind is perverted by fanaticism." He added,

> I believed that my Susie knows me too well to think that I would wish her to marry me if she thought she was violating her principles in doing so. Indeed much as I love you I could not urge it on such terms. I shall never quarrel with my own darling's enthusiasm but at the same time remember that in this world where the feeling mind has so much to suffer, a little *indifference* is also a most useful quality to enable us to pass thro' it in tranquility and make us independent of others who would poison our enjoyments every moment of our lives. But I am encroaching on Mr R's privilege of preaching — would to God that I could act up to my own doctrines. It would have saved me many a bitter pang. (*Letters* 20-21)

Clearly, the engagement made room for Susanna's passionate enthusiasm even as it recognized that her religious feelings were more secular — that is, more literary and humanitarian — than she was wont to admit. She shared with John both "the feeling mind" and a desire for tranquil independence. His awareness of the difficulty of achieving such independence "in this world" no doubt accorded with her own; it made their joint pursuit of that goal all the more attractive to her, for he offered her the perspective she needed to balance her depths of emotional response. In a 19 October letter to James Bird, she praised "the noble chivalrous and poetic feelings" of John's letters, linking them to "the hearts of those who have been reared amid scenes of barren grandeur." Somewhat carried away in her feelings, she claimed that "In spite of the cold I am sure I should be happy with Dunbar anywhere if beneath the burning suns of Africa or building a nest among the eagles of the storm encircled Orkneys" *(Susanna Moodie* 53). Canada was not yet an option for them.

The pressures of change and financial insecurity, however, led to a reversal in late January 1831. Susanna reported to the Birds that she had broken off her "too hasty" engagement. "I will," she wrote, "neither marry a soldier nor leave my country for ever and feel happy that I am once more my own mistress" *(Susanna Moodie* 55). Absorbing herself for the moment in the swirl of London activities and busy with the writing not only of the narratives of Mary Prince and Ashton Warner but also of several book reviews for the *Athenaeum*, she arranged to board in London. Bent now on "try[ing] my fortune in the world of letters," she self-consciously called attention to her venturesomeness and described to the Birds the considerable attention she was receiving:

> Ah! I have seen a great many strangers and have been shown up at Martin the Engravers [the artist John Martin] for a Lioness. I am almost tired with compliments and sick of flattering encomiums on my genius. How these men in London do talk. I learn daily to laugh at their fine love speeches. *(Susanna Moodie* 56)

Her love for John Moodie was, however, too strong to resist his continued attentions. Her sister Catharine cleverly described her state of mind in a letter to the Birds of Yoxford:

"In spite of the warning of her good padre and her South-wold friends to love none but a good man of their church," she wrote, "poor Susie has become a convert to Lieut. Dunbar Moodie" (qtd. in *Letters* 6).

Thus, on 4 April 1831, from the home of "Papa" Pringle, Susanna wed John at St. Pancras Church in London. Thomas Pringle gave her away in a small ceremony witnessed by her sister Catharine and Mary Prince. "I assure you," Susanna told the Birds, "that instead of feeling the least regret at the step I was taking, if a tear trembled in my eyes, it was one of joy, and I pronounced the fatal obey, with a firm determina-tion to keep it." With a touch of humour that James and Emma Bird would have appreciated, she added, "My blue stockings, since I became a wife, have turned so pale that I think they will soon be quite white, or at least only tinged with a hue of London smoke." In the same letter, however, she admitted to the continuing lure of literary company: "there is to me a charm in literary society which none other can give, were it only for the sake of studying more closely the imperfections of temper and the curious manner in which vanity displays itself in persons of superior mind and intellect" (*Susanna Moodie* 61).

The Moodies set up house in London but within months elected to move to a rented cottage in Southwold. Comfort-able in their less costly quarters where they were but "a pleasant walk from Reydon," Susanna experienced the "quiet and rational enjoyments" of marriage, even as she delighted in the familial connections available to her in Southwold (*Susanna Moodie* 62). Plans for the long term were, however, never far from the couple's minds. Indeed, on 31 August she reported to the Birds that "We entertain serious thoughts of going next spring to join my brother in Canada." Having recently received a visit in Southwold from Robert Reid, a prosperous Upper Canadian settler who had become Samuel

Strickland's father-in-law, they were attracted by the prospects he described. Warning the Birds "not [to] be surprised at our flight in the spring," she reported,

> He promises us independence and comfort on the other side of the water and even wealth after a few years toil. This at present he enjoys after a struggle of 12 years and he has now the satisfaction of seeing a family of ten children all in a fair way of becoming wealthy landowners. (*Susanna Moodie* 63)

Robert Reid had emigrated from Ireland to Upper Canada in 1822-23 with Thomas A. Stewart and their families after the failure of a textile business in which they were involved. Granted a large tract of land in the southern part of Douro township, the two Anglo-Irish gentlemen found themselves in a virtually unsettled area just north of the village of Peterborough (which was not yet named) and east of the Otonabee River. Their responsibility was to place settlers on their land grant for a fee, while developing their own farms and water rights. At the same time, they could designate parcels of land to their children. Reid, who quickly proved himself an able settler, could speak with pride and authority about the rewards that followed from such a struggle.

For his part, John Moodie was keenly attentive to what Susanna later called the "Canada mania" that prevailed in England during these months. He had exhausted his hopes "to procure advancements in [his military] profession" and had no familial support he could draw on in Britain (*Letters* 31). With steadily growing interest, he consulted Samuel Strickland's letters home, read as widely as he could about Canada, and, with Tom Wales of Southwold (the feckless Tom Wilson of *Roughing It in the Bush*), attended at least one of the lectures given by William Cattermole in Suffolk on emigration to Canada. Doubtless too he followed Cattermole's additional reports and letters that appeared in the *Suffolk Chronicle* over the winter.

With so much positive information before him and with the pleasant prospect of joining Samuel as a settler near Herriott's (or Nelson's) Falls (the site of present-day Lakefield, Ontario), John Moodie set about consolidating his plans. He worked steadily at his book on South Africa in the hope of being able to leave a completed draft with a London publisher, he raised what funds he could, he sought out letters of recommendation from influential figures such as Lord Lynedoch, under whom he had served in the Netherlands (see *Letters* 30-31), and he booked passage, arranging to visit Scotland with Susanna before sailing to Canada. By February, he already knew that Samuel Strickland had "secured for [him] 146 acres of excellent land fronting a small lake which he says, when cleared, will command an enchanting view" (*Susanna Moodie* 67).

The fact that Susanna was expecting their first child in the spring only increased the necessity of establishing a definite plan. As she reported to Emma Bird on 6 November 1831, "every thing is settled for our emigration" (*Susanna Moodie* 64). Anticipating her confinement with "a secret dread," she added, "I am so happy, so very happy now, that I fear such cannot long exist on earth." Her affection for her husband was rapturous:

> Ah, he is so kind, so good, so indulgent to all my wayward fits, that I look up to him as to my guardian Angel. I seem to lose my own identity in him, and become indifferent to every thing else in the world. "Ah," you will say, this is preaching like a young wife, wait a few years, and then tell me what you think of matrimony. I do not much fear the trial, my heart will never grow old or cold to him. (65)

True to her word, her affection for John Moodie seldom slackened. Missing him while he was away from home in 1856, she told her sister Catharine that "Time lengthens into ages while he is away. Will age never diminish my love for this man — No, thanks to my organs of adhesion and obstinacy. No one can accuse me of being fickle to those I love — for he is as dear to me after five and twenty years of intercourse as he was when we first met" (168).

The baby, Katherine Mary Josephine, arrived on 14 February 1832. Naming her after her sister Catharine, Susanna endured a protracted and painful delivery, the "last seven hours beating all that I ever imagined of mortal suffering." The child, however, was "very fine and healthy" and bore a "truly astonishing" resemblance to "her dear father" (*Susanna Moodie* 66).

The final months that the Moodies spent in Southwold were complicated by an unanticipated development. Catharine returned to Reydon to deliver a double shock to her family. After the failure of her lengthy engagement to Francis Harral, she had stayed in London with her elderly aunt Rebecca Leverton, then had taken a tour with her of southwestern England. But in the meantime, a new plan had been brewing. Not only was Catharine to be married as soon as possible to Moodie's fellow officer and Orcadian, Thomas Traill, but they had also elected to emigrate to Canada, if possible in the company of the Moodies. The Strickland family was much taken aback and displeased by the sudden news. Nevertheless, although they worried about Traill's utter lack of experience as a farmer and his apparent impecuniousness (he had two young sons by his previous marriage who were being cared for in Scotland, and Westove, the Traill family estate, had been encumbered with debt for years), they were no match for Catharine's determination once she had charted her course. Thus, Catharine and Thomas were married on 13 May 1832 in a family ceremony at Reydon Chapel. Two days later, they left for Scotland, weeks before the better-prepared Moodies were booked to sail north to Edinburgh by North Sea steamer.

# CHAPTER 2

# Rough Years in the Backwoods 1832-39

The story of the Moodies' trip down the St. Lawrence River, from Grosse Isle to Quebec (City) to Montreal and then by stagecoach and steamer to Cobourg, is familiar to readers of *Roughing It in the Bush*. Less well known is its prequel, *Flora Lyndsay: or, Passages in an Eventful Life*, which "should have been the commencement of *Roughing It*, for it was written for it": Moodie, however, "took a freak of cutting it out of the MS," thus "beginning the work at Grosse Isle" (*Susanna Moodie* 130). Written in the late 1840s and first entitled "Trifles from the Burthen of a Life" (Moodie valued that title, using it at least twice in her autobiographical writing of this period), the manuscript finally became *Flora Lyndsay* in 1854. Although fictionalized by means of altered names and the use of third-person narrative, the novel is as autobiographical in spirit and essence as *Roughing It in the Bush*. As such, it provides much valuable detail about the Moodies as a newly married couple and a context for Susanna's feelings as she faced the daunting fact of emigration to a distant place. Regrettably, *Flora Lyndsay*, which has never been published in Canada, remains a rare book. Readers wishing to consult it can track down a copy (see the COHM collection) or look at the earlier, less complete, version published as a serial in the *Literary Garland* in 1851 (see *Voyages* 160-240).

When the Moodies sought to embark from Southwold on 31 May 1832, they were accompanied by their daughter, Katie, whom Susanna was still nursing; her troublesome nursemaid, Hannah; and James Bird (James Hawke), the twelve-year-old, "mischievous, laughter loving" son of their close friends, James and Emma Bird (*Flora Lyndsay* 130; all quotations from *Flora Lyndsay* come from the American edition, published as one volume in 1855). Young James was to seek his fortune in the backwoods of Canada under the tutelage of Samuel Strickland. His father was at the leave-taking to present a poetic tribute written for the occasion to young Katie. It would later be included in his collected poems and used by Susanna in the *Victoria Magazine*. Also present were Susanna's longtime Quaker friend from Ipswich, Allen Ransome (Adam Mansel), whose "joyous disposition" and "exquisite taste for music" could "scarcely be trammelled down by the severe conventional rules of [his] Society" (90), and Mary Gooding (Mary Parnell), Susanna's close friend, to whom she dedicated the English edition of *Flora Lyndsay* (94).

The leave-taking occurred under ominous circumstances. The previous night, a change in the weather had brought a heavy storm to the East Anglian coast, and it was still raging the next morning. After much havering by those on shore, conditions were at last deemed suitable to take the party out in a large, open pilot boat to meet the scheduled ship for Edinburgh. At anchor on the rough, dangerous waters of the North Sea, the party waited for ten hours in pouring rain, returning finally to Southwold after nightfall when all hope of the ship's appearance was abandoned. Three days later, according to *Flora Lyndsay*, a second, day-long attempt to meet the Edinburgh ship also had to be aborted because of increasing fog and the ship's failure to appear. Thus, it was only on the third attempt that the weary Moodies succeeded in boarding an Edinburgh-bound ship and beginning their long journey to Canada.

Susanna was seasick during the overnight run to Edinburgh, but her weakness could not undermine her enthusiasm for the "[g]lorious" city she saw for the first time from the deck of the *City of Edinburgh*. Neither was she overwhelmed at this point by her sense of loss in leaving home, because, as she noted, "novelty" or "danger" always made her spirits rise, banishing "useless regrets and repinings" (*Flora Lyndsay* 94). Although she had been much troubled before and during her departure by "bad omen[s]," which she saw as "mysterious presentiments" of "evil" (90), it was characteristic of her to respond freshly to new circumstances and possibilities, once it was clear that her circumstances were altered. Hence, when told by the ship's captain that the sight of "the rock-defended fortress" of Quebec would provide her with "almost as fine" a view as that of Edinburgh, Susanna told him that he had "made [her] quite happy." In terms of "romantic sublimity," she had already decided that Edinburgh had no "equal in the wide world" (125), and she added, "I have contemplated a residence in Canada with feelings of such antipathy, that your description of Quebec almost reconciles me to my lot. I can never hate a country which abounds in natural beauty" (126).

Once in Edinburgh, the Moodies had to alter their plans, for the *Chiefton*, the ship on which they had booked passage for Canada, had already sailed. Accordingly, they boarded with old family friends of John's in Leith, while he took advantage of the delay to work on the final chapter of his book and to arrange a new booking. Given the unexpected luxury of free time, Susanna relieved her loneliness and increasing anxiety by exploring the city with James Bird, observing with him the peculiarities of Scottish manners and enjoying the distinctive accents. He tried to help her climb Arthur's Seat, the first "mountain" that she had ever seen (*Flora Lyndsay* 137). They also walked the tidal beaches of Leith. So taken was she with "that land of poetry and romance" and its "truthful, high-minded, hospitable people" (166) that she wrote, "If I were not English, I should like to be Scotch" (139). She also entertained some of her husband's literary friends near the end of their month-long stay.

It was on one of their walks that Susanna and James made "the important discovery" of a new posting (140). The brig *Anne*, it was announced, would sail on the first of July for Canada. Already very concerned about the grim conditions on board the *Flora*, a ship that John was considering, they relayed the news of an alternative and set about trying to convince him that a change was in order. The *Anne* was a one-masted vessel "resembling a collier"; it had a crew of eight, and it "promised everything but aristocratic accommodations for women and children" (141). Although there were seventy-two booked in steerage, no cabin passengers had been arranged. When the captain, a one-eyed, "rough, blunt-looking tar" (141) named George Rodgers (Ballstadt 554), offered Susanna the small but clean and private "state-cabin," she was even more convinced that they should alter their plans. John, however, was less sure, in part because the *Flora* sailed two weeks earlier than the *Anne* and because he was well aware of the need to be in Canada as early as possible in order to make appropriate arrangements before winter. But in time he was persuaded, largely because of the "mean conduct" of the *Flora*'s owner in his negotiating tactics (*Flora Lyndsay* 145).

As June drew to a close, the much-feared cholera epidemic began to "make fearful progress" in Edinburgh and in the coastal regions of Scotland. Susanna fell ill for a few days, though not with the dreaded disease, as it was initially thought. She was just beginning to recover when the departure of the *Anne* was announced for the next day. After hurriedly packing, the Moodies embarked from Leith at 4 p.m. in a gloomy downpour, without either family or friends to bid them farewell.

As they travelled north, Susanna saw from the deck "the auld town" of Aberdeen, "the dreary Caithness coast," and "the fantastic red rock" of John o' Groats "house" (190), which she had previously imagined to be an actual dwelling; while passing through "the stormy Pentland Firth," she caught a glimpse of Melsetter, her husband's former ancestral home on the island of Hoy (*Flora Lyndsay* 190). The captain chose to take advantage of a good wind rather than stop at Kirkwall for fresh water and supplies, thus depriving Susanna of her chance to visit the Orkney capital and leaving the *Anne* short of fresh water and supplies for the crossing. Once around the northern tip of Scotland, she was awestruck by Loch Girbol and the mountains along the "wild Sutherland coast." Witnessing the "stern sublimity," she felt a "fear" and "a strange madness" that she linked to "the sight of these mountains" and to the fanciful idea that "the earth [here] has rebelled against her Maker and dares to defy Him to his face": "I feel myself grow pale while looking at them, and tremble while I admire" (194). Beyond lay "the immensity of ocean," which she feared would separate her forever from all that she had known and deeply valued (195).

It is perhaps appropriate to pause here to consider the phenomenon that Susanna Moodie represented — and depicted herself as representing — at this moment of intense visual stimulation and emotional departure. Clearly, she saw herself as heir to and representative of the English female romantic sensibility. Eager to embrace beauty and grandeur, and to be their sensitive register, she places herself alone on deck at sunrise. Vividly remembering earlier self-images she had cherished — as a child of the rural Suffolk lowlands and as a young woman attuned to the "mysterious presentiments" of the heart (she called the language of intuition "her favourite theory" [*Flora Lyndsay* 90]) — she reads the rugged landscape of northern Scotland, the first such landscape she had seen, in two languages: her aesthetic of the sublime, and her Christian seriousness. Thus, what she sees is to her "terrific!" — a word that at root combines the fine and the fearful. Her husband, who views her "sensations" as "almost incomprehensible," joins her to serve as her foil. An Orcadian who loves adventure and travel, he sees the "rugged coast" not only as familiar but also as grand and exhilarating (194).

At the same time, her language is precisely that of the woman of sensibility poised between mutually exclusive worlds. Condemned to emigration, Susanna builds her feelings of impending loss into her reading of the landscape. But she is also writing retrospectively, with an awareness of what her family had to face and endure in the process of emigration and pioneering. Thus, she layers her reading with the knowledge that her intuition was correct — her leave-taking was indeed for ever. With an acute recollection of how close she and her family often came to disaster — consider the cholera they escaped in both Scotland and Canada, the fates of the two ships on which they had originally booked passage (the *Chieftain* lost all of its passengers to cholera, while the *Flora* [strategically renamed the *Rachel* in *Flora Lyndsay*] was wrecked off Newfoundland after twelve weeks at sea and the occurrence of a mutiny [342-43]), and their later trials in the bush and in Belleville — she heavily freights her "sense

of loneliness, of perpetual exile" (195), as she retires to the
solitude of her cabin to "bewail" the loss of her native land.
That mood she would often recall and nurture "amid the dark
woods of Canada" (194). Retrospective knowledge would,
however, also provide the justification for her confidence
that a caring God was watching over her family, somehow
steering them through the dangers that beset them. Always
effusive when she felt emotional response was called for, she
superimposes her faith in "that protecting and merciful inter-
position, so often manifested by the Great Father to his
dependent children," upon the evil thoughts and doubts that
often affected her in the immediacy of those dangers and
problems. The result is a proclamation of sorts: a conviction
concerning the specialness of her "August destiny," and a
celebration of the part that destiny has allowed her to play in
the spirit of progress (343).

After a promising start, the ocean crossing of the *Anne* was
long, uncomfortable, and tedious. Indifferent winds and a
foggy becalming off the Banks of Newfoundland extended
the voyage from six weeks, the maximum period for which
the ship was provisioned, to nearly eight weeks. The lack of
food and fresh water — the "dead, corrupt" water from Leith
had not been replaced at Kirkwall (319) — led to strict
rationing after only three weeks at sea and caused increasingly grave worries about survival for those on board. For her
part, because of a "severe indisposition" and her weakened
condition, Susanna found it necessary to wean Katie (Josie).
While her daughter flourished thereafter without her "natural sustenance," Susanna herself battled exhaustion on a diet
of oatmeal and twice-daily spoonfuls of port provided by the
captain (327). As well, in the close quarters of the cabin
passengers, unanticipated problems and antagonisms arose.
Hannah, for instance, engaged in a conspicuous flirtation
with the captain, which led to words between him and John

Moodie and a mood of mistrust and sulking in Rodgers thereafter. The rebellious Hannah, who virtually withdrew her services as Katie's nursemaid during the crossing, proved a liability both on board and later in Canada; it was an understatement to say that she "occasioned [Susanna] much anxiety and uneasiness" (206).

There were also bad feelings among some of the cabin passengers. Indeed, Susanna devoted part of *Flora Lyndsay's* second volume to a dramatization of these tensions. In particular, she focused on the antics of the rascalish Mr. Lootie, a stowaway, complainer, and artful gambler who seems to be a parallel figure to the little stumpy man of *Roughing It in the Bush*; another stowaway named Stephen Corrie, whose good-hearted nonchalance suggests the characterization of John Monaghan; and a puritanical minister who, after fanatically condemning the captain for fishing on the Sabbath, accepted a cod caught on Sunday for his own meal without a further word of reproach. She filled out the volume by including a story entitled "Noah Cotton," which she claimed that she had written at sea to "divert her mind from dwelling too much upon the future, and [to] interest her husband" (215).

When the crew finally sighted Cape Breton on "a warm, delicious summer evening, . . . the smell of the pine forests . . . was as rich as vales of Araby to the poor emigrants" (334). That very night, however, they were beset by a sudden and powerful offshore storm that imperilled the ship and made sleep impossible in the thoroughly drenched cabin. With the captain "out of his reckoning altogether," John Moodie stayed up all night, taking his turn at the wheel and, with several sturdy men, managed to keep the *Anne* off the rocks by turning her out to sea (see 337). John was seldom at a loss, Susanna learned, when danger loomed. The next day, they were again on course aided by a fast-running ocean. Three days later, on 25 August, they reached Cape Rosier, where to everyone's joy they took on fresh provisions and a pilot to guide them up the St. Lawrence.

The delight of crew and passengers was quickly chastened by "fearful intelligence": "the cholera was raging in Quebec, and spreading into the Upper Province" (337). The rest of the trip to Grosse Isle, where the ship had to undergo mandatory medical inspection at the newly established cholera station, was marked by Susanna's first Canadian thunderstorm and her opportunity to observe the beauties of the river landscape. Never had she beheld such "awful and terrific beauty" as during that storm, with its "electric flashes of blinding light" and "ear-splitting peals of thunder." Aware that the ship's cargo included gunpowder and informed of the devastating forest fires that such storms sometimes caused, she spent yet another uneasy night on board the *Anne* (340). The next day, however, she clung to her post on deck drinking in the "noble panorama" of the wide river and imagining "its chains of inland seas" as subjects of artistic representation. With the perspective of many years in Canada, she wrote:

Perhaps no country in the world could present finer subjects for such a work, with water so pure — skies so blue — rock, mountain, and forest so vast — and cities, towns, and villages along its shores placed in such picturesque and imposing situations. A pictorial map of Canada could alone give a just idea of the beauty and importance of this great country to the good folks at home. Then consider the adjuncts of such a landscape — the falls of Montmorency, and God's masterpiece, Niagara. The panorama of its Upper and Lower Mississippi would lose half its beauty, when contrasted with the panorama of the St. Lawrence, with its tumultuous rapids and thousand isles. (341)

Again, Moodie's vision invokes the now and then, integrating a knowledge of things seen later with the glories of a landscape already manifesting the colourful signs of autumn's approach.

## INTO THE INTERIOR:
## FROM GROSSE ISLE TO COBOURG

The *Anne* anchored at Grosse Isle on the morning of 30 August. In choosing to begin *Roughing It in the Bush* with their arrival there, Susanna Moodie exercised a shrewd dramatic sense. The primary feelings that characterize its opening are fear and worry, not the relief felt at the conclusion of the long voyage in *Flora Lyndsay*. The initial words — "The dreadful cholera was depopulating Quebec and Montreal, when our ship cast anchor . . ." (21) — set a Poe-like mood of impending doom. The presence of death at the gates of freedom was daunting.

The real concern at Grosse Isle was, of course, to arrest the spread of the contagion from Europe, a danger augmented by the unsanitary and crowded conditions endured by most steerage passengers on route to Canada. While Moodie acknowledged the importance of that work, she placed her emphasis on the feelings of alarm and uncertainty that immigrants, especially sensitive female immigrants like herself, felt in arriving in a strange, beautiful, but dangerous place. Thus, she juxtaposed images of death and thoughtless (or excessive) behaviour with scenes of beauty and pathos, wringing all she could from what had been a time of fear and concern for her family and herself, as well as an occasion of tremendous visual and aesthetic stimulation. When inclined to be carried away by her daydreams inspired by the beauties of the landscape, she was checked by experienced travellers such as the *Anne's* captain. He told her, "Don't be too sanguine, Mrs. Moodie; many things look well at a distance which are bad enough when near" (28).

The ship, a prison in the latter stages of *Flora Lyndsay*, thus became an "ark of safety" (56) in the events Moodie described in the first two and a half chapters of *Roughing It in the Bush*. By its means, those on board kept away from the dangers around them and were guided past the cities of Quebec and Montreal, which seemed so attractive and pleasing from a distance. While Quebec, perched fortresslike atop Cape Diamond, immediately replaced Edinburgh as her *"beau idéal . . .* of all that was beautiful in Nature" (37), she was much disappointed to hear some of the steerage passengers who went ashore describe it as "a filthy hole" (42).

After dropping off some passengers there, the *Anne* proceeded to Montreal, arriving on 3 September. There Moodie did go ashore and she was most impressed by the shocking advances of the epidemic. At each turn of the street, there was a reminder that "death was everywhere" (55), and, as one gloomy excise officer told her, "It will be a miracle if you escape" (51). She learned that all the sewers had been opened "to purify the place and stop the ravages of the pestilence"; as a result, "the public thoroughfares [were] almost impassable," and the air was "loaded" with "intolerable effluvia" (51). Returning to the ship, the Moodies discovered that their "ark" had become the site of a case of cholera and thus of potential quarantine. With their stagecoach trip westward already arranged, they hurriedly left the ship and took overnight rooms at Goodenough's Hotel.

By a combination of stage and boat, the Moodies travelled via Cornwall to Prescott, where they boarded the *William* iv. After a stop at Kingston, they sailed overnight through a storm to the "pretty rising village" of Cobourg "pleasantly situated on the shores of Lake Ontario" (*Life* 173), where they sought accommodation amid a crush of immigrants and travellers of various classes. After some negotiation, they managed to book rooms at Strong's Steamboat Hotel. There they would stay for three weeks while John Moodie investigated for himself the relative advantages of settling close to Lake Ontario ("the front") or of taking up the grant of land that Samuel Strickland had arranged for them near his own homestead in the backwoods forty miles north of Cobourg. Although Strickland was awaiting their arrival, and although Catharine and Thomas Traill had already passed through Cobourg on their way north, John was unconvinced that the struggle to clear heavily treed land in the backwoods was the best option available to his family in Canada. When he had an opportunity the next day to witness the back-breaking effort to clear and drain "a thick cedar-swamp" adjacent to the village, he was struck by the hopelessness of the task. "My heart," he recalled, "almost sickened at the prospect of clearing such land" (*Roughing It* 225). An experienced farmer in South Africa, he could readily assess the high costs of labour, money, and time involved in such undertakings.

Another factor in his thinking was the experience reported by his friend, the feckless and amiable Tom Wales (*Roughing It*'s Tom Wilson), whom they chanced upon at the Steamboat Hotel. Having shared John's plan to emigrate, Tom had left Suffolk early in the spring and had bought a farm in Douro township, the very destination originally settled on by the Moodies. His time and effort, however, had been almost entirely unproductive, and he had returned to Cobourg with little to show but his comical horror stories, enough money for his return passage, and a bear that he called his only Canadian friend. At the same time, John befriended the hotelier, Owen Strong, "a truly excellent and obliging American" (*Roughing It* 221), and other travellers and locals he met there. Strong welcomed his plan to settle nearby and helped him in his search for an affordable farm in the vicinity.

While her husband was thus involved, Susanna endured her "unpleasant" residence in the crowded "house of public entertainment" as best she could. With leisure and conveniences available to her but often alone with Katie while John was farm-hunting, she found herself "daily yielding up my whole heart and soul to that worst of all maladies, home-sickness" (*Life* 173). Her mood was such that she was too lonely and dejected to engage in new writing. "Memory," she told a female friend, "is my worst companion; for by constantly recalling scenes of past happiness, she renders me discontented with the present, and hopeless of the future, and it will require all your kind sympathy to reconcile me to Canada" (174).

Despite Susanna's dejection, writing was never far from her mind. It is a curious anomaly of her literary life in Canada that several poems, some from *Enthusiasm, and Other Poems*, had appeared in the Cobourg *Star*, the leading newspaper of the area, nearly a year prior to her arrival in town. They included "The Vision of Dry Bones" (20 September 1831) and "Elijah in the Wilderness" (18 October 1831) and were likely passed on to the editor, R.D. Chatterton, by Robert Reid or Samuel Strickland. Later in the autumn of 1832, other poems from her published volume also appeared in the newspaper — for example, "Lines Written Amidst the Ruins of a Church on the Coast of Suffolk" (19 September), "Uncertainty" (31 October) and "Youth and Age" (19 December). John, who had one of his own prose pieces published in the Cobourg *Star*, served as her connection. Although her opportunities in Upper Canada would be fewer and her connections much more limited than in London, Susanna was, even in her homesick state of mind, eager to keep up her literary reputation and place her name before the people of the colony.

The one event that Moodie herself dramatized from her

sojourn at the Steamboat Hotel appeared in the *Literary Garland* (February 1851) and *Life in the Clearings versus the Bush* under the title "Michael Macbride." It proved to be one of her most controversial pieces, arousing the anger of several Irish editors in Canada who saw her as "evidently ignorant of all the genuine characteristics of that fine people." Indeed, the criticism of George Edward Clerk, the editor of the (Montreal) *True Witness and Catholic Chronicle* (21 February 1851), led her to pull the story from its appropriate place in *Roughing It in the Bush* (*Susanna Moodie* 109). For her part, Susanna was genuinely startled by the hostile reaction. As she told her Montreal publisher, John Lovell, in a letter dated 1 March 1851, the "deathbed scene of Michael Macbride is strictly true"; the story's subsequent events had been corroborated by "a person whose veracity I never heard doubted" (*Letters* 217), and it had been "written years ago, without a thought that it could give offence to any party" (218). Such political naïveté would often confound and disturb Susanna during her career as a writer in Canada.

While at the Steamboat Hotel, Susanna heard of a penniless young Irishman who was dying of consumption in another part of the building. Raised for the priesthood by an uncle in Peterborough, Michael Macbride (not his real name) had wanted to be a farmer and had developed some hostility to the strict Catholic discipline forced upon him. Denied his inheritance by his uncle (ostensibly as a result of his obstinacy), he had struggled to make his own way despite failing health and lack of funds. The humane Owen Strong had taken him in, well aware that he was dying. Upon the arrival of Macbride's mother from Ireland (her own crossing providing a cautionary tale of emigration), a pitched battle on religious grounds had begun around her son's bed. She wished her son to be looked after by a priest, while Michael himself insisted on receiving a Protestant clergyman. Urged by a female friend at the hotel to read the Bible to Michael while his travel-weary mother slept, Susanna did as requested. When the mother awoke and intervened fiercely, condemning the Protestant "trash" that Susanna was reading, Susanna was able to convince her that she was only following Michael's request. In such crucial matters, she argued, "The Bible is its own interpreter," and the "question of creeds" is not at issue (*Life* 179).

Years later, having had the Peterborough part of Michael Macbride's story confirmed and amplified by a disinterested third party ("Mr. W —," who was likely a Peterborough merchant), Moodie remained fascinated by the event and convinced of the appropriateness and correctness of her actions and interpretation. Nor did she doubt the need for *"real* Christian *charity* and *mutual forbearance"* in human relations (*Letters* 218). What she did not anticipate was the hostile Irish reaction to a narrative that presumed that a Catholic on his deathbed would, or could, accept Protestant consolation. The editor of the *True Witness and Catholic Chronicle* attacked her for her gall and presumption: "For shame! Bible-reading authoress! — how could you get an unfortunate scape-grace who had been a Catholic, to believe that your reading of some select chapters could supply to his soul these tremendous wants?" (qtd. in *Susanna Moodie* 109). What the self-righteous Mr. Clerk blithely overlooked in his indictment was the fact, clearly presented in the narrative, that Macbride had long since and for his own reasons renounced his Catholic connections. The reception of his story proved, however, a sharp introduction into the religious and racial intolerance that characterized life in Upper Canada. As certain reviews of *Roughing It in the Bush* indicate, Moodie was seen by Irish journalists in Britain and Canada as an Irish-basher who needed appropriate chastisement. She, of course, never saw herself in such a light, and she failed to anticipate the extent to which her unqualified observations might provoke hostile responses.

In seeking reliable, objective advice about farming opportunities, John Moodie found himself obliged to rely for the most part on land-jobbers or real estate salesmen, men who frequented the hotels and generally played upon the ignorance and eagerness of recent immigrants. Most of the local farmers were also caught up in "the rage for speculation and trading in land" (*Roughing It* 229) and thus were too interested in their own opportunities to be much trusted. When it became clear to Moodie that he lacked the capital to buy any of the more eligible farms near Cobourg, he thought that he might get a good farm "at an unusually low price" if it were in the interests of a land-jobber to trade on his "respectable" character in order to improve the market value of other properties that the jobber controlled (233). Beguiled by the "remarkable" character and apparent thoughtfulness of one such merchant and land-dealer, Charles Clark (Q. in *Roughing It*), Moodie decided to deal with him (233). Thus, he paid his upper limit, three hundred pounds ("certainly cheap at the price" [236]) for a well-situated, two-hundred acre farm west of the village. It included an extensive orchard, two log houses, and a frame barn. Located on Gage's Creek in Hamilton Township, eight miles west of Cobourg and four miles east of the smaller village of Port Hope, it was situated near the York [Toronto]-Kingston road and was sufficiently cleared to allow for immediate and productive farming.

The problem was that, unknown to Moodie, Clark did not own the property. Rather, he held a mortgage against the owner, Joseph Harris, as security for debts owed to his Cobourg store. Having an interest in getting "rid of a set of Yankee rascals who prevented emigrants from settling in that neighbourhood," he was, however, eager to induce Harris to sell the land to Moodie through him. Clark managed to

convince him — likely for a fee or a trade — to part with the
farm. Twenty years later, Moodie was still "unable to tell
by what means [Clark] succeeded in getting Mr. H[arris] to
part with his property" (236). However, there was a further
catch that the "free-and-easy" Clark downplayed (235). The
Harrises would not be able to leave the farmhouse on such
short notice. The land-jobber's solution was simple; for the
short term, the Moodies would rent at "the *moderate* sum of
four dollars a month" a small log house near their property
(89). So quickly was this plan devised that John had no
chance to see the dwelling.

Moodie should have been more suspicious. Certainly, in
retrospect, he pinned considerable blame on Clark for other
problematic investments he made a few years later. And
he recalled, rather self-protectively, his initial hesitancy in
dealing with such a "cunning" man, one whose "heart was
case-hardened" and whose "conscience [was] like gum-
elastic" (234). However, Clark's smoothness, the apparent
advantages of the deal, and the lateness of the season all
conspired against hesitation and second thoughts. The purchase of Lot 32, Concession 4, was thus effected, and the
Moodies made their plans to move as soon as possible to
Gage's Creek. They left Cobourg on 22 September with Tom
Wales, who was too weak with the ague to return to England,
in their party.

It was verbally agreed that Joe Harris, his pregnant wife,
Hannah, and their eight children would not have to leave
the farmhouse until "the commencement of sleighing" (88).
Meanwhile, the Moodies would camp for the rest of the
autumn in what turned out to be "a miserable hut" nearby.
Travelling in the rain by wagon from Cobourg, they arrived
with all their goods only to find "not a house, but a cattle-
shed, or pig-sty" (90). Moreover, it was doorless and dirty,
with a single broken window. Thus began their struggles in

their first Canadian "Home," struggles that comprise the first half — that is, the first volume — of *Roughing It in the Bush.*

## HAMILTON TOWNSHIP AND
## THE YANKEE SQUATTERS

The Moodies stayed in Hamilton Township for eighteen months, living in three different residences during that period and enduring an almost constant antagonism from the local "Yankee" residents. While they outlasted most of them over that period, they nevertheless decided to move north to their Douro land grant in February 1834. That move, as both John and Susanna would often recall, was the major tactical error in their settlement plans. They would have been far better off to stay where they had begun to establish them-selves, close to Lake Ontario and the many opportunities available along the front.

Having made the "untenable tenement" liveable, the Moodies, along with Tom Wales and Hannah, made do at close quarters (91). Those early days were punctuated by intrusions from the Seaton family (or families). Roswell Seaton, or, as Susanna called him, Old Satan, was a local reprobate with a record of court appearances. He was one of the targets of Charles Clark's cleanup campaign, for which the Moodies were the advance guard. It was in fact Old Satan's cabin that they were renting, though part of the money was likely going directly to Clark, who had Seaton firmly in his debt and was only awaiting an opportunity to foreclose on and sell his property.

Manifesting an almost proprietorial interest in the new ten-ants, the Seaton family — Emily in particular — was quick to introduce the Moodies to the vagaries of the "borrowing system," a means of sharing resources between settlers for mutual benefit and support. The Seatons, however, had no desire to share; rather, they sought to take as much advantage as they could of the alien newcomers. For his part, Tom Wales took delight in frightening the superstitious Roswell. The roots of the confrontation lay in the smouldering animosity that existed between Americans (in this case, "late Loyalists" such as the Seatons and Harrises living in Upper Canada) and newly arrived, inexperienced British immigrants. The contempt felt by these "Yankee rascals" for the superior airs of the British was matched by the disgust people like the Moodies directed at the dishonest practices and the contempt for education and manners that in their eyes characterized the ne'er-do-well, illiterate, and presumptuous locals. It was a standoff of opposed value systems.

Late in the autumn, while still awaiting the realization of Joe Harris's "many fair promises of leaving the residence we had bought, the moment he had sold his crops and could remove his family," the Moodies were again visited by Charles Clark (127). This time he arrived with another English gentleman in tow as a prospective purchaser of the property (Lot 30, Concession 4, Hamilton Township) on which Roswell Seaton had been living for years. "Captain S —" (Captain Francis Shea) from Demerara (Ballstadt 570) was phase two of Clark's improve-the-neighbourhood plan. With winter fast approaching, things were unfolding much as Clark had hoped (*Roughing It* 127). He concluded the deal on the spot during a dinner Susanna arranged and hosted. As a result, the Moodies found themselves with only a week to relocate.

Again Clark was quick with an ad hoc solution that served his larger purposes. The land-jobber made arrangements for the Moodies to take over what was the second, and very small, residence on the Harris farm. This was the "log hut" where the mother of Joe Harris lived alone (129). "[T]hat old witch," as Clark called her, despised her son's wife and kept a deliberate distance from her family (128). Promising the Moodies that their stay would "only be for a week or two, at farthest," Clark cleverly negotiated ("cajole[d]" was his word) an agreement whereby (128), for the exorbitant fee of twenty dollars, the Moodies would take over her "ruined old shed" (131); for her part, she agreed to cancel the dowry right she still held on the property that she and her husband had settled thirty-six years earlier, an important detail Clark had heretofore neglected to address (133).

In early November, Susanna left "Old Satan's hut without regret, glad, at any rate, to be in a place of my own, however humble" (134). Nevertheless, the Moodies paid a stiff price, both financially and in terms of inconvenience, for the opportunity to be further disadvantaged. In practical terms, however, there was little they could do but keep their part of the various agreements into which Clark had led them. Appeal to the law would have been too slow a process, and the Moodies knew too little of local customs to be sure of how to proceed. To make matters worse, Tom Wales had recovered sufficiently to sail for England before the winter closed in. His departure increased their loneliness but at least gave them more room when space was at a premium.

The "week or two" in old Mrs. Harris's "odious, cribbed-up place" lasted the entire winter of 1832-33 (163). Not only were the Moodies distressed by Joe Harris's continuing excuses for not moving; living now on the gentle slope a mere stone's throw from the Harris farmhouse, they were also "never free from the intrusion of Uncle Joe's wife and children" (135). Joe explained that he could not move immediately because his wife was pregnant, turning a blind eye to the fact that Susanna herself was evidently pregnant. Rather, he relished the chance to have revenge on both the Moodies and Clark, though it was only the former who suffered. For their part, the Moodies were hesitant to create a row, dependent as they often were on their neighbours for advice and help.

For the Moodies as a family, "the iron winter of 1833" was a trial of unexpected discomfort and strain. The problem of heating a small cabin and cooking in it without risking a fire or discomforting all those inside was not easily mastered. With considerable candour, Susanna acknowledged the hard lessons of that first uncomfortable winter when she noted that "the rigour of the climate subdued my proud, independent English spirit, and I actually shamed my womanhood, and cried with the cold" (144). She likely felt that shame on numerous occasions. At the same time, the hostility of the Harrises was exacerbated by the actions of the Moodies' new servant, John Monaghan, who had arrived at their door in a snowstorm that first winter. Because of their unusual circumstances, the Moodies and Harrises had to share the same barn for both feed and cattle. Accordingly, Uncle Joe's opportunities to disadvantage John Moodie were many. The impetuous and loyal Monaghan was not hesitant to call Joe's bluff when he caught Joe in the act, and on one occasion, according to *Roughing It in the Bush*, Harris angrily struck Monaghan over the head with a pitchfork.

The animosity between the families grew as the winter unfolded. The bothersome and impertinent visits of the Harrises were, according to Susanna, "not visits of love"; rather, she saw them as motivated by "mere idle curiosity, not unmingled with malicious hatred" (135). Much as Susanna was often genuinely amused by Joe Harris's antics and language, she felt deeply betrayed by the Harris women, from whom she had hoped for more sympathy and fellow-feeling, especially given her family's patience in waiting out Joe's promises. Her only friend among them was the "very handsome" fourteen-year-old Phoebe Harris, who became seriously ill in March 1833, likely with pneumonia (160).

Relying on the lore of the local women, Hannah Harris
refused to seek medical help for her eldest daughter, whom
she assumed would recover in due time. At Phoebe's request,
however, Susanna introduced the girl to some of the Christian ideas she had missed in a home that didn't want "to know
anything about Jesus Christ here" (161). Risking "the men-
aces of the heathen mother" (161), Susanna "felt a powerful
interest in [Phoebe's] fate" and arranged to read the Bible to
her as often as she could (162). She insisted on being the girl's
missionary in the face of her mother's rudeness and impiety.
While Hannah Harris "did not actually forbid [Susanna] the
house, . . . she never failed to make all the noise she could to
disturb [her] reading and conversation with Phoebe" (162).

A subtle but compelling undercurrent of *Roughing It in
the Bush* concerns Susanna's need for a trusted and intimate
female companion. She had had several such friends in Southwold. In Hamilton Township, no special companion emerged
for her — only a set of women who disappointed her expectations in one way or another and violated her values and
sense of decorum. Hannah Harris's campaign of hostility
disturbed her on a daily basis, and she could find no warmth
at the Harris house. The potential she noted in Betty B (she
was both "original" [107] and "remarkably civil" [106], though
of scandalous reputation) and in proud old Mrs. Harris ("she
was really possessed of no ordinary capacity, and, though
rude and uneducated, might have been a very superior person under different circumstances" [140]) also suggests her
hunger for stimulating or elevating friendship. Indeed, volume 1 of *Roughing It in the Bush* is conspicuously lacking in
agreeable female companions of Moodie's own class. Her
narrative interest is directed instead to those eccentric and
problematic male figures she knew: Tom Wilson, Brian B —
(Brian Bouskill, who finally succeeded in taking his own life
in 1838), Old Satan, Joe Harris, and John Monaghan.

The Moodies did make the acquaintance of numerous couples of their own class in Hamilton Township and Cobourg, but among them no woman seems to have emerged as a special friend for Susanna. Those mentioned are usually unnamed and receive a cool presentation. A newcomer to the area, Moodie brought with her a reputation as a writer that seems to have isolated her all the more and increased her nervousness and self-consciousness among other gentlewomen. In "The Charivari," she noted that Cobourg society held literary people in "supreme detestation" (201). She found herself suspected of being the next Mrs. Trollope, a writer who, with sharp satiric strokes, would use her experiences to mock and scorn the provinciality and decorum of polite, unsuspecting Canadian society. "I tried," Susanna recalled, "to conceal my blue stockings beneath the long conventional robes of the tamest commonplace." The result, she felt, was a restraint on her conversation that was mistrusted and criticized as "stand-aloofishness." "Oh, yes," women would whisper; "she can write, but she can do nothing else." In the end, with few allies and much disappointment, Susanna "gave up all ideas of visiting them" and, stung by the ill-informed judgements of her domestic incapacity, and the advice she received from her "self-constituted advisers" she became "more diligent in cultivating every branch of domestic usefulness" (201-02).

On the last day of May 1833, the Harrises finally left the house for the Rice Lake plains. Joe, however, made sure that he left his signature as nastily as possible. He hid a skunk in a cupboard in the house so that the smell would haunt the Moodies long after his departure. Quickly disposing of the offending animal, the Moodies, along with John Monaghan and their new servant, Bell (Isobel), cleaned up the mess that was left and moved in, a full seven months after the date Harris had originally promised. The house was overrun by mice (they trapped fourteen the first night) and fleas, as well as by large black ants that lived in the old logs, and they had much to contend with by way of adaptation. Susanna helped in that process by naming the farm Melsetter after John's Orkney birthplace. It was there on 9 June that she gave birth to Agnes Dunbar, her second daughter. From there a few days later, she saw a group of mourners carry the body of Phoebe to be buried in the Harris plot near the creek, which separated the two domiciles that were the fundamental locations of the story of her first winter in Canada.

The remaining eight months of the Moodies' stay in Hamilton Township were likewise unpleasant, though less immediately bothersome. Many of the Yankees had moved away — the Seatons during the winter and the Harrises by June — so that the intrusive borrowing and inquisitiveness were largely at an end. What made them uncomfortable now followed from the deal that John Moodie had arranged, again on the basis of "very reasonable" and disinterested local advice (168), to help them with the burden of farming. He had contracted with a likely couple, "the O—s," to farm Melsetter on shares for a twelve-month period. Although Susanna gives less emphasis to the role this family played in their increasing dissatisfaction with the area, a close look at *Roughing It in the Bush* indicates the pain she personally felt as a result of her frequent contacts with Mrs. O—. Again a sense of betrayal — woman to woman — animates Moodie's comments about this "generally . . . most unwelcome visitor" with "her gossiping, mischievous propensities" (207). Of Mr. O—, she reported that, "had the man been left to himself, I believe we should have done pretty well" in the arrangement; his wife, however, was "a coarse-minded, bold woman, who instigated him to every mischief. They took advantage of us in every way they could, and were constantly committing petty depredations" (168).

The O—s receive no sketch of their own. Rather, Susanna uses parts of "Phoebe H —, and Our Second Moving" and "The Charivari" to depict this troubling relationship. Her earliest comments pinpoint the extent of the blame she ascribed to them. "From our engagement with these people commenced that long series of losses and troubles to which their conduct formed the prelude" (168). The O—s moved into old Mrs. Harris's shack and proceeded, as the summer unfolded, to cheat and disadvantage the Moodies with regard to the produce, especially when John was away (168). Mrs. O— was brazen in her defiance of Susanna's objections. At the same time, the O—s proved an "irksome [social] restraint." In Susanna's words,

> We had no longer any privacy, our servants were cross-questioned, and our family affairs canvassed by these gossiping people, who spread about a thousand falsehoods regarding us. I was so much disgusted with this shareship, that I would gladly have given them all the proceeds of the farm to get rid of them. . . . (169)

In "The Charivari," Mrs. O— becomes one of the mouthpieces of thoughtless prejudice and failed standards of human conduct, the kind of behaviour Susanna despised, especially in women who, she felt, should have known better.

But while life at Melsetter remained discomforting and lonely for Susanna, and while the respectable women of Cobourg and area showed little interest in her, she began to look more widely for literary opportunities. Beyond the space that editors usually reserved for the "Poet's Corner" in local newspapers, the Moodies could see that there were few opportunities available in Upper Canada. Bookmaking was still an unusual undertaking in the colony. When opportunities did arise, however, they were ready for them.

Pieces of Susanna's writing appeared in two short-lived York (Toronto) magazines of 1833. The first, entitled the *Canadian Literary Magazine*, was edited by John Kent under the patronage of the lieutenant governor, Sir John Colborne. Four items of her prose and poetry, including "Oh, Can You Leave Your Native Land. A Canadian Song" and "The Convict's Wife: A Sketch," appeared in its three issues before it folded for lack of sufficient subscribers. An "inferior" effort called the *Canadian Magazine* also appeared in 1833 but lasted only two issues (*Life* 289).

Not surprisingly, Susanna's best opportunities at this time proved to be American and English. The first was Dr. John S. Bartlett's (New York) *Albion*, a popular newspaper that featured the latest in Old World news and current literature. Moodie wrote to Bartlett on 14 February 1833, introducing herself as a writer "deemed not unworthy of public notice in my native land" and enclosing two poems, which she described as "the first flight of my muse on Canadian shores" (*Susanna Moodie* 90). Bartlett published her "Song: The Strains We Hear in Foreign Lands" and "The Sleigh-Bells. A Canadian Song" in the paper's 2 March issue. Although he confused Susanna with her older sister Agnes in his introductory note, he later clarified her identity and published more of her poems. "There's Rest," which Moodie claimed she wrote while on the St. Lawrence, appeared in the 25 May 1833 issue. A year later, Bartlett published a poem that would be much reprinted in later years, "The Canadian Herd-Boy" (28 June 1834), and he inserted a few of her poems into his other paper, the *Emigrant* (New York) — for instance, "The Canadian Woodsman" (25 June 1834). So enthusiastic was he about the Moodies as a writing couple that he urged them to move to New York, where he would do all he could to aid them; in fact, he suggested that Susanna become a regular contributor (*Susanna Moodie* 216).

Back in London, her sisters Agnes and Elizabeth sought to find outlets for her work. Through Eliza, who had a position with the *Lady's Magazine*, Agnes arranged the publication of several of Susanna's pieces, including poems written in Canada, such as "What Is Death?" (February 1833) and "Music's Memories" (January 1834). She also shopped around certain stories that Susanna had either left with or sent to her, and she offered literary advice, sometimes rather naïve, to both of her sisters in Canada. Impressed by the large sales of Charles Knight's *Penny Magazine* in Britain, she urged Susanna and Catharine (though they lived many miles apart in a fledgling colony that had virtually no audience for the literary) to start up a similar venture in Upper Canada.

Agnes's surviving letters to Susanna (see the Patrick Hamilton Ewing Collection at the National Library of Canada) provided her with a wealth of literary news. Agnes reported on her own busy comings and goings in London and passed on warm greetings from or news about various London and Suffolk literary figures (Leitch Ritchie, John Martin, Godwin, and Pringle). Interestingly, insofar as Agnes's missives refer to Susanna's letters home during this period, they indicate that they were generally positive in tone and spirit. In a letter of 15 April 1833, for instance, Agnes reported that, while she "grieve[d] that you should be the tenants of a comfortless hut and exposed to so many hardships and privations," the family at Reydon "have few pleasures that are more gratifying to us than the receipt of your affectionate and interesting letters affording us as they do such pleasing accounts of yourself, Moodie and the sweet sweet baby." Agnes was very fond of little Katie and John Moodie; she affectionately dubbed him "the Chief" and occasionally wrote to him as a friend (see Agnes's letter of 25 February 1834). Her letter of 21 October 1833 to Susanna also alludes to "the good accounts you have given of yourself[,] brother Moodie and the dear babies" of your life in Canada and makes mention of the suffering and "long tedious getting up you had" in giving birth to Agnes the previous June. The difficulties that Moodie had in her pregnancies are seldom mentioned in *Roughing It in the Bush*, but they should not be overlooked in any contemporary reading of her life. Astute readings of the maternal aspects of Moodie's autobiographical writing appear in essays by Bina Freiwald and Helen Buss.

### BACKWOODS DIARY, 1834

Although the Moodies later came to regret their decision to leave Hamilton Township for the backwoods and Lake Katchawanook, the available evidence suggests a kind of inevitability in their choice. Caught in a disagreeable twelve-month obligation to the O—s, lacking congenial society to lighten their domestic burdens and loneliness, and having a potentially valuable grant of land in Douro that required proving-up if they were to keep it, John Moodie travelled north to Douro in the summer of 1833 to confer with Sam Strickland about his options. Impressed by the progress being made by both Sam and his old friend Thomas Traill, he also liked what he saw of the area's potential. The water system that decades later would become the Trent-Severn Waterway — a means of linking Lake Ontario (at what is now Trenton) with Lake Huron and the far west — was about to be surveyed, and, given the completed work on the Welland and Rideau Canals, there was growing optimism that property along its route would soon increase significantly in value. Economic conditions seemed propitious, and immigration, despite the continuing threat of cholera, remained high. As a further incentive for moving north, John and Sam agreed to work jointly as agents promoting land sales to British investors. Sam's continuing links to the Canada

Company (he had been involved in the development of the Guelph and Goderich settlements) and Moodie's Old World connections provided the basis for their fledgling collaboration.

Having decided to move to the backwoods, John Moodie negotiated to expand his holdings on Lake Katchawanook. Over the next few months, he bought two adjacent lots, giving him "a compact farm of three hundred and sixty acres . . . which was amply sufficient for the comfortable subsistence of a family, had matters gone well with me" (*Roughing It* 253). It was located on the east side of the lake, which was really a widening of the Otonabee River between present-day Lakefield and Young's Point, a mile north of the Traills and about two miles from Sam's homestead. Determined that Susanna and his daughters would this time have an adequate home to move into upon arrival, John contracted to have a log house constructed in his absence. He was aided in his transactions by the news of an inheritance of seven hundred pounds that came to Susanna as a consequence of a relative's death in 1833. About the same time, he also decided to sell his half-pay pension (the bulk of which he invested in stock in a Lake Ontario steamer called the *Cobourg*) and the Hamilton Township farm. Again Charles Clark was his agent, and again, in regard to both the stock and the farm, Clark seems to have managed things to his own advantage. The *Cobourg* stock proved a bust, as once again events outstripped Moodie's plans. What seemed to be a solid investment that would pay Moodie more annually than his fixed pension proved a liability when a litigious wrangle between the boat's principal partners kept it out of the water for most of the 1830s.

On a bright, frosty morning in early February 1834, the Moodies moved north with all their belongings packed in two wagons. After an arduous day and night of travel in which they passed near the Cavan swamp and Susanna saw the town of Peterborough for the first time, they struggled along the "bad" road north of town in the darkness, hoping to reach the Douro backwoods and the kindly welcome of Sam and Mary Strickland before midnight. The trip ended depressingly for Susanna as she not only suffered a blow to the head but also had much of her china broken in a late-evening accident. Crossing the rickety bridge at Herriot's Falls (Lakefield), the only bridge over the Otonabee north of Peterborough and one that would be swept away that very spring, she looked forward to her arrival at her brother's. However, her "first halt in that weary wilderness" proved all too brief (270). Circumstances required that they continue on to the Traills, where they were at last heartily received by her sister and brother-in-law.

Susanna Moodie's introduction to the backwoods was disconcerting and distressing. Beyond the exhausting journey, she found the dark overarching forest particularly foreboding. We must remember here that the landscape she experienced was different from what a visitor would see today. Gone are the white pines that towered above the cedars and birches, and gone are the densities of forest growth — the bush, as she called it — that challenged the early settlers. It is not surprising that images of despondency and darkness preoccupied her as she travelled north. Despite her disappointments with her neighbours and the quality of social life in the Cobourg area, she had become attached to Melsetter and, in this sense, was resistant to a change of locale, even if it meant proximity to her sister and brother. When a February thaw followed their arrival, the world outside became "a murky haze" (273), a "cheerless waste" (274): "The charred and blackened stumps on the few acres that had been cleared during the preceding year were everything but picturesque, and I concluded, as I turned, disgusted, from the prospect before me, that there was very little beauty to be found in the backwoods" (274).

Her "jaundiced eyes" were soon cured (274). With the experience and cheerfulness of her sister to guide her and an improved view of their prospects as encouragement, she found herself becoming less timid in her outings and more reconciled to her new home. While Susanna slowly adapted herself to her new circumstances, Catharine began to write — on speculation — a book about her personal experience of emigration and settlement (*The Backwoods of Canada* would be published in London in January 1836), perhaps inspired in part by her efforts to introduce her sister to life in the woods and the strategies best suited to it.

The first months that the Moodies spent in Douro proved to be a pleasant, upbeat experience. The spring and early summer were their "halcyon days of the bush," a time of "comparative ease and idleness" in which they explored the area by land and water (278). Susanna noted with pride that she became "quite a proficient in the gentle craft." Canoeing and fishing held a great appeal for her; indeed, her skill in fishing helped to sustain the family when times became tough and resources were few (279). While John oversaw the clearing of sections of their land and they worked on their garden, the Moodies became familiar with the local Chippewa (Mississauga) families who camped near their clearing. They engaged in bartering, exchanged visits, and shared useful information when the Chippewa were hunting and fishing in the area.

The summer of 1834, which Susanna called "the hottest I ever remember," was altogether different — a period memorable for its dangers and discomforts (305). Not only were she and her daughters briefly trapped and terrified when a hired boy inadvisedly set fire to the fallow surrounding the house just as the wind was rising, but in July, though she

Moodies' Douro property showing the site of their dug well, c. 1909.
PHOTOGRAPH BY GEORGE DOUGLAS. COURTESY KATHERINE HOOKE.

was in the late stages of her third pregnancy, she was required to host three logging bees as a means of clearing sixteen acres of forest for their fall wheat. Her comments on these "noisy, riotous, drunken meetings" — she called them "the most disgusting picture of a bush life" — are one of the most remarked upon features of *Roughing It in the Bush* (313-14), an index of both her moral outrage and her desire for privacy.

Then, in late August, with much harvesting and planting to be done, the whole family came down with the ague, the malarial lake fever or "shaking mania" that had prostrated Tom Wales the previous summer (77). The pronounced heat of the season no doubt increased the strength of the mosquito population and thus the frequency and virulence of the disease. Its effects were intermittent, but it lingered for months and was a principal bane of the pioneers in Upper Canada. In this instance, the whole community around Herriot's Falls, including the Stricklands and the Traills, was likewise affected.

Under these conditions, and having recently lost her reliable female servant, Susanna endured the last uncomfortable weeks of her pregnancy. With her daughter Agnes near death (in her view), she gave birth at home to her first son, John Alexander Dunbar (Dunnie) on 26 August, then was deprived of her nurse, who, overcome by ague, was carried home by her husband the following day. Alone with her newborn boy, an "insensible" daughter, and an ailing husband, Susanna endured what she called "a melancholy season, one of severe mental and bodily suffering" (323). The blandness of her phrasing masks her real anguish, particularly what she meant by severe mental suffering. Not only was she weakened by the birth, but she also fell victim soon after to the debilitations of the ague. Recollecting those dark and depressing days, she concluded:

Those who have drawn such agreeable pictures of a residence in the backwoods never dwell upon the periods of sickness, when, far from medical advice, and often, as in my case, deprived of the assistance of friends by adverse circumstances, you are left to languish, unattended, upon the couch of pain. (323-24)

Here, as in several other places, Moodie implicitly juxtaposes the warnings that *Roughing It in the Bush* presents with the more cheerful but fundamentally misleading picture of pioneering life offered in her sister's *The Backwoods of Canada*, a book that covers much the same period — in this instance, 1834 — but opts to overlook the personal suffering and pain involved. More importantly, this depressing season was but a prelude to the physical and mental anguish Moodie would endure during her last winter in the bush. These two troubling periods — the summer of 1834 and the winter of 1839 — were the bookends of her education in suffering and her exploration of personal limits.

So strong was the grip of the ague that it hung on in the Moodie family until late in the spring of 1835. But in the face of so much discomfort and immobilization, what such periods revealed to the Moodies was the true value of their servants and friends. During their bush years, Jacob Faithful (as they called him after the title character in a popular novel of 1834 by Captain Marryat), John Monaghan, Mary Pine (Payne), and Jenny Buchanan were most helpful and loyal. In particular, Jacob's ministrations to them during the worst of the ague were "marked with the greatest kindness and consideration" (325). While the Stricklands and the Traills could offer little help at the time, Lt. Alexander and Charlotte Emilia Shairp and Lt. Col. John and Hannah Caddy, who lived north of the Moodies' clearing, were similarly generous in their help and much concerned about the

Moodies' welfare. Indeed, while Alexander Shairp, in the absence of his wife, provided some thoughtful aid to the Moodies at this time (325), Emilia became Susanna's closest and most valued friend. During these months (and years), there may even have been something of a rivalry between Susanna and Catharine for Emilia's friendship and attention. Certainly, Emilia's proximity and companionship added greatly to Susanna's emotional comfort during these years.

## 1835

Overall, 1835 was a better year for the Moodies. The ague had run its course by late spring, and enough land had been cleared to allow for substantial sowing and planting. With a year's experience behind them, the Moodies acclimatized themselves more completely to the demands of their new situation, though John remained uncertain about whether he wanted to commit himself and his family to the backwoods. Thomas Traill must have had similar reservations, for he was advertising his farm for sale by the summer of 1835. Personal adaptation thus proceeded apace, even as, in ways external to the rituals of the Moodies' backwoods life, forces were at work that would undermine their steady efforts. In Peterborough and environs, hopes ran high about the prospect of a canal system because N.H. Baird had completed and submitted his authorized survey. However, as the months passed by and the government in Toronto showed little interest in committing large sums to the project, a mood of tentativeness and uncertainty overlaid the local optimism.

On the literary front, the Moodies were elated to learn that John's two-volume book, *Ten Years in South Africa*, had finally been published by Richard Bentley in London. More importantly, it was receiving positive reviews, often in conjunction with Thomas Pringle's memoir, *African Sketches* (1834). They were deeply saddened, however, to learn that Pringle, their great friend and supporter, who had been ill for many months, had died late in 1834 shortly after his book had appeared.

While a few of Susanna's poems appeared in the *Albion* ("Human Changes" on 17 January 1835 and "My Native Land" on 24 January), Dr. Bartlett also succeeded in awakening the interest of the still restless John Moodie in a new emigration venture. Beginning in late October 1834, the *Albion* carried advertisements for the Colony of the Rio Grande and the Texas Land Company, a settlement project of "Empressario Dr. Beales" in which Bartlett had an investor's interest. Early that winter, John wrote to Beales's New York secretary, Charles Edwards, offering to serve as literary observer and historian for the settlement in return for a salary, passage for his family, and a land grant. Without his board's approval, Edwards could only promise passage and the guaranteed purchase of "a liberal number of Copies of any work you might write upon the Country." It was, he added, "A Country . . . which no scientific man has written about: — perhaps, the only spot in the world upon which a book has not been perpetrated" (qtd. in *Letters* 12).

Susanna's reaction to this scheme is nowhere recorded, but it is most unlikely that she would have been enthusiastic about moving to the remote southwestern Texas territory, an area plagued by military antagonisms with Mexico. Difficult as the summer and fall of 1834 had been, another major change in her domestic circumstances and the prospect of increased isolation were scarcely the sort of opportunities she would have welcomed. At any rate, Edwards could not get his board's approval to offer Moodie the salary he required, and his letter of 3 March, generous and complimentary as it was, likely dampened John's enthusiasm. In 1836, however, Dr. Beales himself wrote to John, asking his help in encouraging Upper Canadian settlers to join his Texas venture.

By then, apparently, John had more fully committed himself to staying in Canada. For years it would seem he played with alternatives. Despite his Texas inquiries, for instance, he had written a public letter (published through the Canada Company in London and dated 24 November 1833) in support of emigration to Upper Canada. This was likely part of his scheme with Sam Strickland to interest British investors in wild lands (see *Letters* 34-38). Although little seems to have come of that venture, on 9 November 1834 he wrote to Richard Bentley in London with a new idea. His first question for his publisher was whether or not his South African book would in fact be published; his second sought to gauge Bentley's interest in a book about settlement in Upper Canada. Bentley was not enthusiastic. Although he offered to read the manuscript, he felt that "so much has lately been written on that country" to assure a sufficient audience (qtd. in *Letters* 13). His response chilled the project; hence, the seed that would become *Roughing It in the Bush* remained dormant for over a decade.

In the midst of such scheming on John's part, Susanna received a second opportunity to have her writing published in the United States. It came from Sumner Lincoln Fairfield, an Anglophilic American poet based in New England. Fairfield, who edited the *North American Magazine*, had visited "the vast and beautiful Canadas" in 1833-34 and had discovered her poetry while there. In the December 1834 issue, he published a highly complimentary review of *Enthusiasm, and Other Poems* that included the texts of three poems. Effusively, he called her "an honour to the continent which she has selected for a home" and linked her to "that beautiful and brilliant constellation" of female writers that included "the celebrated Hemans, Baillie, Norton, Jameson, Howitt and Shelley, of England." Grandly, he pledged himself "to contribute to diffuse the reputation of this lady" (qtd. in *Susanna Moodie* 75-76).

True to his word, Fairfield included some ten pieces of her poetry and prose in subsequent issues. In November 1836, however, he lost control of the magazine. Notable among his inclusions are a poem about the Moodies' courtship ("Lines: On a Bunch of Withered Flowers, Gathered on Hampstead Heath, and Presented to the Author, by J.W.M., in the Spring of 1830 [July 1835]) and "Home Thoughts of an Emigrant" (November 1836). In a thank-you note to Fairfield from the backwoods (23 January 1835), Susanna enclosed a signed copy of *Enthusiasm, and Other Poems* (which he had already reviewed) and a couple of new poems. However, she regretted that paying the postage to send more material "to such a great distance" was "beyond my means." Besides, she added, with three children to care for, her time was "too valuable to waste in the pursuit of fame"; "a Bush Settler has no 'hours of idleness'" (*Susanna Moodie* 93).

It was during the summer of 1835 that the Moodies took the canoe trip described in *Roughing It in the Bush* north on Lake Katchawanook to Francis Young's mill. Canoeing still farther north to the top of Clear Lake with two of the Young boys, they enjoyed their first view of the unsettled wilderness. Susanna was thrilled by a scene of "wild and lonely grandeur" (337) as "the whole majesty of Stony Lake broke upon us at once" (338). From a point of view on the water — a setting appropriate to her taste and sensibility — she makes clear her abiding affection for a landscape that she initially found daunting and depressing. Katchawanook, she remarks, though far less spectacular than Stony, "was *our* lake, and, consequently, it had ten thousand beauties in our eyes, which would scarcely have attracted the observation of a stranger" (328). No longer an alienated "stranger," Moodie writes with a local pride and a firm sense of belonging.

Happy as such holiday-like outings were for the Moodies, the reality of their daily life had more to do with the stagnation of larger economic forces over which they had no control. Immigration had fallen off dramatically, and money was becoming increasingly scarce in the backwoods. The "very wet" summer of 1835 extended through September and "totally spoiled" their wheat crop, as it did those of most other settlers in the area (351). This loss was a huge blow, for a good harvest was the short-term goal of their investment and labour. Because most of their money had been spent in clearing the land and developing the farm, they were, without a crop to sell, virtually penniless. Caught in a situation in which their very subsistence depended upon their ability to make do with what was available, they adapted themselves to their circumstances. Susanna "worked hard in the field" alongside John (352); she learned new strategies in food preparation, from the making of eel stews to dandelion coffee (a recipe for the latter, which she found in the *Albion*, pleased her so much that she taught it to her Indian friends); and she fished for food in Lake Katchawanook, which her children nicknamed "Mamma's pantry" (356).

In *Roughing It in the Bush*, Susanna describes how her proud resistance to what she at first regarded as degrading work soon altered with experience. Once she was fully engaged, she came to value the satisfactions that followed from demanding labour. It "was not after all such a dreadful hardship," she notes; indeed, on occasion it provided "great pleasure." The analogy she uses to explain her change of outlook is telling: "I have contemplated a well-hoed ridge of potatoes on that bush farm, with as much delight as in years long past I had experienced in examining a fine painting in some well-appointed drawing-room" (353). For Moodie, who always felt it necessary to keep up her genteel outlook for both her readers and herself, such work meant a dramatic revision of her self-image; it meant, in terms appropriate to her established values, an embracing of poverty as a school of "soul-ennobling" self-knowledge and Christian awareness, not of "seeming disgrace" and social failure (352). Her high-toned language, in her mind necessary to appeal to the English readers she sought to address, may put off some contemporary readers and blur for them the simple fact that she became an effective worker who enjoyed the effort and gained by its stimulation. The backwoods were her testing ground as a rounded human being in a new and democratic country. Although the democratic vision she gained must seem limited by twentieth-century standards, it involved a major transformation in personal values, one that bespeaks the positive effects of what John Moodie evocatively imaged as "the rough towel of democracy" (240).

In her study of Moodie's writing, Carol Shields has noted that the presentation of genteel poverty "always requires an accompanying covering statement" (60). The experience of physical work — relentless and exhausting fieldwork — did not make Moodie into a coherent social analyst, a New World proponent of self-discipline or hard-nosed individualism. While she embraced her new self-knowledge with a passion that was consistent with her liberal views concerning race, prejudice, and education, she was no Benjamin Franklin, no Ralph Waldo Emerson. Her personal reformation did, however, awaken her to her place and role in a large and important social transformation that was essentially English Canadian. That she dressed up her role in the Victorian finery of fatedness and untoward destiny was a part of her essence. It required an apologetics addressed to her "genteel" audience — a firm "I'm-really-one-of-you" assurance — even as she asserted her testimonial to the deeper truths she had learned about herself and other human beings, regardless of received views. She was in this sense a work in progress.

Inherent in her apologetics/testimonial was what Shields calls an "ambivalence about the working class" (61). What ambivalence there is, I would suggest, lies less in a failure of vision than in the dynamics of Moodie's evolving sense of herself. For while she had the satisfaction of providing subsistence for her family and gaining self-knowledge by her labouring, she also realized that her identity was rooted elsewhere and could not be fundamentally altered. She was an English gentlewoman with a clear sense of her rightful social position. She would thus function like a member of the working class only as long as it was absolutely necessary. She would not, however, forget what she had learned in doing so, and that learning would feed her vision of Canada as a country evolving — like herself — in a new and better way. The evolution included a movement beyond the restrictions inherent in the English class system, but in a way that was less radical and threatening than the outright republicanism of the United States, a system that she continued to fear even as she learned to value individual Americans the more she had actual contact with them.

## 1836-37

As "Disappointed Hopes" makes clear, the struggles that extended from late 1835 to the rebellion in December 1837 were uninterrupted. Debts incurred in the confident expectation that the *Cobourg* steamboat stock would "realise an income" became a nagging anxiety (353) in a family without much hope of income (*Roughing It* 353). The major depression that stalled development in the Western world from late 1835 through 1837 — and led to the rebellions in both the Canadas — brought economic stagnation to the remote parts of Upper Canada. All the Moodies could do was persevere, living on what the farm and lake provided. They were embarrassed that others should know of and witness "our dreadful struggles with poverty" and "the strange shifts we were forced to make in order to obtain even food" (396). In her treatment of these years, Susanna focuses attention on her loyal and resilient servants — Jacob Faithful, Mary Pine (Payne), and latterly Jenny Buchanan — though the Moodies' inability to pay a wage led at last to Jacob's leaving and their taking in Jenny Buchanan only when she had been summarily and unfairly turned out by her former employer, Captain Frederick Lloyd (Captain N) of Dummer. Susanna's warm regard for Canadian-born servants and well-adapted workers was rooted in these supportive relationships.

In *Roughing It in the Bush*, the years 1836 and 1837 are also distinguished by the presence of two long-term guests, first Malcolm Ramsay, the problematic "little stumpy man," and in his wake the likeable John E— (Evans). The nine-month stay of Ramsay, a disgruntled and self-centred felon of genteel upbringing and distinguished family, preoccupied Susanna's imagination long after he vanished from Douro, for he represented a troubling personal challenge, a male-oriented, clubbish view of life that conceded little place to the views and values of women. He expected to enjoy his friendship with John without her intervention and to be waited on in ways appropriate to a guest of superior background.

For her part, Susanna saw herself as an equal partner in the Moodie family enterprise and did not take lightly the presumption that she should accept a secondary role. Proud of her domestic resourcefulness, she ran the household as best she could during those stressful months, enduring not only the presence of her unwanted guest but also the latter stages of her fourth pregnancy. Donald, her second son, was born on 21 May 1836. But if her resources were limited, so was her patience, especially when it came to certain aspects of Ramsay's behaviour and his sharp judgements of her. The unfairness of his criticisms of her meals and of what he called her prudish and "methodistical" values galled and disturbed her, haunting her memory for decades after he vanished abruptly from their life (372). By his very presence, Ramsay set at odds Moodie's self-consciousness and feelings of failure with her struggle to validate her sense of personal accomplishment and self-development. His judgemental presence stimulated her validation of her progress as a struggling pioneer.

By contrast, John Evans spent about the same length of time with the Moodies and was a welcome, helpful addition to the family. He joined them in the severe winter of 1836-37, shortly after they nearly lost their home to a chimney fire (see "The Fire" in *Roughing It*), and he brightened their dark days considerably. "We were always cheerful," Susanna reports, "and sometimes contented and even happy" with Evans as their boarder and partner. "Our odd meals became a subject of merriment, and the peppermint and sage tea drank with a better flavour when we had one who sympathised in all our trials, and shared all our toils, to partake of it with us" (396).

Although Evans brightened their days and helped with the farming, what the Moodies needed above all was some definitive means of changing their circumstances, of breaking the circle of constraint and bare subsistence in which they found themselves trapped. That opportunity came with the outbreak of the rebellion. In early December 1837, while John Moodie nursed a broken foot he had contrived to splint on his own, the populace heard the stunning news that an armed rebellion had occurred in Toronto. The proclamation of the lieutenant governor of Upper Canada, Sir Francis Bond Head, calling for volunteers to put down the insurrection, went from hand to hand in the backwoods. Despite his injury, Moodie, like many other loyal settlers, set out for Toronto to offer his support in the name of the young queen.

## 1838

Although John Moodie arrived too late to be immediately involved, he managed to gain an official appointment as a captain in a new regiment, the Queen's Own of Toronto, called up in late December 1837 to aid in the defence of Upper Canada's borders. His orders were to outfit himself and report to Toronto for training exercises as soon as possible. Thus, he departed from the farm on 20 January 1838. As a result, Susanna was left alone with only Jenny Buchanan and the four children. John Evans had returned to Ireland to claim a family inheritance, and help was very scarce, even had the Moodies been able to afford it.

What followed was a test of her management skills, enterprise, and stamina, a test that, for the six months of John's absence, Susanna passed with considerable success. Having already endured trials by fire, water, air, and earth during her backwoods experiences, she once again had to rely upon and observe her own resources and capacities. A letter from Thomas Traill to John Moodie — dated May 1838 — testifies glowingly to the capability and worth of John's "most excellent wife":

> Your wife deserves all you say of her. She has commanded the esteem of every one. Your spring crops are nearly in. . . . In fact she is farther advanced than her brother or me, or indeed any of the neighbours. . . . I am happy to say that all your children look fat[,] fair and flourishing as do mine, and you will find on your return which I hope will be soon that every thing has been managed admirably in your absence. . . . (qtd. in *Letters* 95)

How much Susanna was able to write during these years is debatable. She noted in *Life in the Clearings versus the Bush*

Sir George Arthur

that she composed most of *Roughing It in the Bush* while ignorant of life in the towns and villages of Upper Canada. It is evident from dates of publication that she wrote most of the poems that accompany the book's sketches while in Hamilton and Douro townships. By contrast, the sketches are too complex and distanced in their perspective to have been written in these months. She was, however, painting when time allowed and, in a letter to her husband, noted that she had found a market in Peterborough for bird and flower images painted on maple tree fungi (*Letters* 141). She may also have experienced a sense of the limits of her personal energy, feeling herself too used up by household and family demands to undertake late-night writing that would not likely find an outlet. Under the circumstances, poems may have been easier to undertake than prose.

What is clear is that, in the late fall of 1837, with unrest simmering in the Canadas and reports of rebellion increasing, Susanna had begun to write a number of patriotic poems emphasizing loyalty to Britain and Queen Victoria. The first of them, "Canadians, Will You Join the Band — a Loyal Song," appeared in the opening issue of Charles Fothergill's new Toronto newspaper, the *Palladium of British America and Upper Canada Mercantile Advertiser* (20 December 1837). Dated 20 November in Douro, the poem was quickly reprinted in at least eight other places, including John Lovell's Montreal Transcript. Following this poem with several others written over the winter and spring that John Moodie (in his military movements) was able to place with Fothergill in Toronto, she effectively brought her name before an aroused public. "On Reading the Proclamation Delivered by William Lyon Mackenzie, on Navy Island" (17 January 1838) and the better-known "The Burning of the Caroline" (October 1838) are important examples (for the Mackenzie poem, see Ballstadt, "Secure").

The consequences were significant. First, Susanna caught John Lovell's attention in Montreal. A year later — that is, early in 1839 — Lovell wrote to her, inviting contributions for pay to his ambitious new magazine, the *Literary Garland*, and even guaranteeing payment of postage (417). Second, her poems came to the attention of the new lieutenant governor of Upper Canada, Sir George Arthur, who arrived in the province in late March 1838. He seems to have known about her through her published writing prior to receiving a plaintive private letter from her that June, petitioning him to find a military or civil position for her husband, whose six-month appointment to the Queen's Own was to terminate later that summer (424). The connections to Lovell and Arthur eventually proved instrumental in allowing the Moodies to escape the "green prison of the woods," (*Life* xxxii) to which economic circumstances and ill luck had condemned them.

John Moodie's Queen's Own appointment allowed the Moodies to liquidate half of their debt to the Jorys of Dummer (423), for services on the farm, and to meet other pressing needs. But while his return to the farm in early August signified an end to his precious source of income, it reunited him with Susanna, whose main concern during his long absence had been her loneliness without him. Although she had carried on capably and without complaint during his absence, she had found life a burden without him. Thus, with John Evans back from Ireland and eager to lend his support, the family enjoyed "the happiest [harvest] we ever spent in the bush":

We had enough of the common necessaries of life. A spirit of peace and harmony pervaded our little dwelling, for the most affectionate attachment existed among its members. We were not troubled with servants, for the good old Jenny we regarded as a humble friend, and were freed, by that circumstance, from many of the cares

George, Baron de Rottenburg.

COURTESY THE ARCHIVES OF ONTARIO (S14583).

and vexations of a bush life. Our evening excursions on
the lake were doubly enjoyed after the labours of the day,
and night brought us calm and healthful repose. (425)

The conjunction of repose and health is indicative of the
calm and satisfaction that Susanna felt in the presence of her
husband. Note too the intimate feeling for the land they
shared in such moments. The memory of that good season
together, however, would stand in sharp contrast to the
struggles that lay ahead for Susanna during the long winter
of 1838-39, struggles that put a dark and painful stamp upon
her backwoods experiences.

With autumn giving way to winter, two events occurred
that further brightened the Moodies' happiness and immediate prospects. First, on 16 October Susanna gave birth to
their third son and fifth child, John Strickland. A few days
later, by her own account, her husband received a letter
appointing him "with the rank and full pay of captain" as
"pay-master" to the several militia units serving the north
shore of Lake Ontario from Trenton to Bath. "This," reported
Susanna, "was Sir George Arthur's doing. He returned no
answer to my application, but he did not forget us" (436).
Doubtless, she was right in her reading of the sequence of
events. Her thank-you letter to Arthur (18 December 1838)
and his comments in later letters to John Moodie make it
clear that he was concerned for and personally interested
in her situation (see Peterman, "Susanna Moodie and Sir
George Arthur").

## 1839

With John departed for the Victoria District to work under
George de Rottenburg, a former secretary to Arthur, Susanna
and Jenny again settled into the lonely routine of the farm in

winter. The rationale for the separation was practical: given that there was no assurance of an appointment beyond six months, John would be able to earn more against their debts by not undertaking the expense of removing his family to Belleville. Susanna's confidence in her ability to weather another six months is implicit in the thank-you letter she sent to Sir George Arthur a week before Christmas. Rather than emphasizing her own needs, she devoted most of her available space to imploring his help for her sister Catharine — her sister "in misfortune," as she called her — who was in bed recovering from the birth of her fourth child and coping under circumstances that she was sure would shock the lieutenant governor. In Catharine's case, however, Arthur could not or did not find a position for Lt. Thomas Traill (Peterman, "Susanna Moodie and Sir George Arthur" 135).

Letters that Susanna wrote not only to Arthur but also to her absent husband are crucial components in understanding her state of mind and the problems she encountered during her final full winter in the backwoods. In particular, the correspondence between Susanna and John (25 December 1838 to 16 July 1839) while he was posted in Belleville provides an evocative description of her trials, which is especially important because, in *Roughing It in the Bush*, she is remarkably reticent about these months. Only two paragraphs describe them, one at the end of "The Whirlwind" and one at the beginning of "A Change in Our Prospects," and they are separated by a misplaced chapter, "The Walk to Dummer," which describes an event that took place during the previous winter; accordingly, readers may easily miss the connection between the paragraphs and the emotional significance of her limited commentary on this winter of "severe trial" (436). Those events cast a dark shadow over her imagination, a shadow that she could not escape when she came to write her account of those years.

Cross-written letter, 1839.

The problems began with her breast-feeding of Johnny. By Christmas, Susanna had developed a breast infection that confined her to bed for more than a week. Lying "like a crushed snake on my back" and in "great agony," she finally sent for Dr. John Hutchison in Peterborough, though she continued to feed her son. So advanced was her mastitis that it might well have proved fatal had Hutchison not come the twelve miles through the bush to lance her breast and drain it of the poison. To John she wrote two weeks later,

> You may imagine what I suffered when I tell you that more than half a pint of matter must have followed the cut of the lancet, and the wound has continued to discharge ever since. I was often quite out of my senses, and only recovered to weep over the probability that I might never see my beloved husband again. (*Letters* 114)

For his part Dr. John Hutchison was shocked by the conditions in which he found her. With "great emphasis," he told her, "In the name of God! Mrs. Moodie get out of this" (114).

Hutchison was a well-seasoned witness to shocking situations and the firmness of his reaction is suggestive. Reduced to inactivity by the mastitis, Susanna had no one but Jenny Buchanan to turn to, and Jenny's abilities were not of a delicate nature. Thus, her situation — what she called "the discomforts and miseries of Douro" — must indeed have appeared forlorn to her (116). Still, she tried not to let her medical condition or the gloom of her circumstances undermine her discipline. As she reported in the same letter (11 January 1831), she was on her feet again, though in a weakened state, seeing to domestic matters, dealing with the deep cut her son Donald had suffered when he had fallen headfirst into the stove, and weighing alternatives to staying in the bush all winter. "But," as she confessed to John, "I must try to be contented, but sickness has tamed down my spirit. I seem no longer able to contend with my comfortless situation and the charity of my kind neighbors really distresses me" (116-17).

Susanna was in a decidedly upbeat mood in her Valentine's Day letter of 14 February. She was cheered by the receipt of John's affectionate letter, her returning strength, and the news that he had finally sold his South African farm in the Groote Valley. Still, she mentions that she and the children "suffered dreadfully from cold" because they did "not dar[e] to put much fire into the stove on account of the bad pipes" (124) and that she had come to the aid of her neighbour, Hannah Caddy, nursing her through a serious abdominal illness when, as was so often the case in the backwoods, no doctor would come up the twelve miles from Peterborough.

In *Roughing It in the Bush*, Susanna mentions an epidemic of "malignant scarlet fever" that threatened her two daughters for three weeks and then, as a result of anxiety and fatigue, rendered her "perfectly helpless" for "nearly ten weeks." That, she claims, was followed by an illness to the baby that Dr. B — (Dr. George G. Bird of Peterborough) "pronounced mortal" (436). Again, the effect on her was powerful: "these severe mental trials rendered me weak and nervous, and more anxious than ever to be re-united to my husband" (436-37). Her letters, however, do not mention the scarlet fever that so endangered Katie and Agnes, and it is possible that, in writing the sketch years later, she mistook the precise occasion of that epidemic, just as she misplaced "The Walk to Dummer" in the chronology of their experiences.

Whether or not the girls were seriously ill in 1839, it is clear that, for Susanna, the spectre of disease dominated her later memories of that winter. In her letter of 6 March to her husband, she describes in harrowing detail how first Donald and then Johnny were struck by "this horrible influenza"; no doctor would come up to the bush, likely because of the

pressing needs in Peterborough, where several children did
in fact die during the epidemic. With Johnny in a kind of
coma and possibly near death, the elderly Dr. Bird did
journey north from the town and told her, after looking to
the boy, "that without medical aid the child must have died"
(*Letters* 131). Susanna added that, though she herself had been
ill as a result of the anxiety and nursing, she had followed
Dr. Bird's receipts and was better.

No illness of note is mentioned in her remaining letters
other than a bout of ague that came in April and by May left
her weak and "as yellow as a piece of parchment" (147). What
persisted in its stead were her growing loneliness, enervation,
and anxiety, fed by worry about debts, an increasing sense of
obligation to friends who had temporarily adopted Dunbar
and Agnes, and her own impatience to be reunited with her
husband. Doubtless too her loneliness was exacerbated by the
departure of the Traills, who had at last sold their Douro farm
in February, and the continued absence of her close friend
Emilia Shairp, who had moved to Peterborough to open a
school when her husband returned to England to pursue his
naval career.

Susanna's monthly letters ring out with her affection for
and need of her husband, both emotionally and physically. In
her 6 May letter, she spoke of the painfulness of "these long
separations," adding that "A state of widowhood does not
suit my ardent affections" (147). She also teased him about
his ability to guess the exact size of her foot: "No wonder —
you know it so well, for surely if any man ever knew how to
please a poor silly women [sic] 'tis yourself'" (146-47). On
their wedding anniversary, she shared with him a dream she
had enjoyed — a dream that speaks legions about their
lovemaking and intimacy. "I dreampt you returned last
night," she told him, "and I was so glad, but you pushed me
away, and said you had taken a vow of celebacy [sic] and

meant to live alone, and I burst into such fits of laughing that
I awoke" (141).

As for her writing, there was as yet little movement. Having
received John Lovell's invitation to contribute to the *Literary
Garland*, she had sent off a poem or two but by 14 February
had received only a copy of the first issue, which she judged
"a wretched performance," though the typography and paper
were good. Somewhat ingenuously, she noted: "I must say, I
do not much like being the lioness of it" (128). Although two
of her poems — "The Oath of the Canadian Volunteers: A
Loyal Song" and "The Otonabee" — appeared in the May
issue, the payment Lovell had promised was not immediately
forthcoming. Despite her desperate need for cash to meet
pressing debts, she could only wait patiently. In her letter of
1 June, Susanna told John that Lovell had promised five
pounds for work she had sent but that as yet she had received
nothing (153); on 16 July, she again reported that "I have
been disappointed in receiving the money I expected from
Montreal" (158). Hence, the great literary offer that had
brightened her days and "opened up a new era in my exist-
ence" did little to provide relief when she most needed it in
early 1839 (*Roughing It* 417).

Susanna's letters to John conclude with a missive of deep
anxiety dated 16 July. Not having heard from him for more
than a month and every day anxiously awaiting his return,
she criticized his cruelty in keeping her in "this dreadful state
of uncertainty" about his plans and movements (158). Her
spirits had finally reached their nadir; "I am so dispirited,"
she wrote, "that I care nothing about [the farm]" (158). "Oh
heaven keep me from being left in these miserable circumstances another year," she told him (158-59).

Such another winter as the last will pile the turf over
my head. I cannot help crying when I think, that such,

may be in store for me. While I had you to comfort and
support me all trials seemed light, but left to myself, in
this solitude, with only old Jenny to speak to, and
hearing so seldom of you makes my life a burden to me.
(159)

Their letters, it would appear, crossed in the slow mail
service of 1839. His note — dated 5 July — reached her
shortly after she had sent her lonely cri de coeur. In it, John
explained to his "Dearest Susie" the military-related reason
for his delay and gave her the good news he had recently
received (155). On Baron de Rottenburg's urging, he had
written to Sir George Arthur to inquire about the shrievalty
of the newly named Hastings County (formerly the Victoria
District). By return mail (26 June), Arthur's secretary had
promised that, "not only on your own account, but from the
esteem and respect he entertains for Mrs. Moodie," the
lieutenant governor would "avail himself of the first possible
opportunity of complying with your desire for employment,
and thereby gratifying his own anxiety to render some service
to your interesting family" (155-56). De Rottenburg assured
Moodie that he could count on Arthur's promise. For all his
continuing debts, John could thus cautiously rejoice in the
prospect of better times ahead; he and Susanna would soon
"see an end to our troubles and again take our proper place
in Society, from which we have been so rudely jostled by our
adverse fortune" (156).

John returned to Douro in August, having paid off several
of their debts, and together he and Susanna gathered in their
"scanty harvest." But it was now possible to look "less to the
dark than to the sunny side of the landscape" (*Roughing It*
475). In the early fall came Sir George Arthur's promised
letter appointing John as sheriff of Hastings County. Again
he set off for Belleville, this time to make his personal

arrangements for the sureties (personal financial guarantors) required for his position and to find a home for his family. His letter of 24 November, however, sets out some of the dangers he saw awaiting them in a town very much polarized by strong party feeling and religious denomination. "We shall have a difficult part to perform here," he told her, "but by steadily pursuing a conciliatory course to all I trust by the blessing of God we may be the means of doing much good" (*Letters* 161). Thus, it was into a tense and danger-filled political environment that Susanna moved when, at the end of December 1839, with the help of her brother Sam, she, her children, and Jenny travelled by sleigh to Belleville to begin their new life.

# CHAPTER 3

# Belleville and Its Perils

## A SHERIFF'S LIFE IN THE CLEARINGS

Susanna Moodie arrived in Belleville with the new decade. On one level, certainly, the town must have been a sanctuary to her, a bustling Lake Ontario port of fifteen hundred inhabitants that represented for her family not only a fresh start but also the possibility of a social life such as she could only have imagined in the Douro woods. Moreover, John's new position assured a status for them, even though they were conspicuously outsiders. Yet ever resistant to changes of locale, Susanna was nervous and reticent about her new life. The bush had aged and weathered her considerably: "I looked double the age I really was, and my hair was already thickly sprinkled with grey." Having "lived out of the world entirely" for seven years, she found herself clinging to her "solitude" and "obscurity," feeling "no longer fit for the world" and unprepared to enter into a range of demanding activities with people she did not know (*Roughing It* 476).

Despite "the great beauty of the locality," Belleville proved to be a considerable disappointment on first glance; it was, in 1840, "but an insignificant, dirty-looking place" (*Life* 29). Perhaps expecting too much after her long exile, Susanna was disappointed by its muddy streets and irregular houses, and as well as by the lack of taste, neatness, and colour in its layout. In fact, the town was but slowly emerging from the effects of the same depression and military-related constraints that had burdened the Moodies in the backwoods. However, as Susanna was quick to add, in the twelve years between her arrival and the appearance of *Roughing It in the Bush*, there had been "a wonderful, an almost miraculous, change in the aspect and circumstances of the town." The population had tripled, the town site had doubled, and handsome commodious stores and large hotels had replaced "the small dark frame buildings" that had characterized the place in 1840 (*Life* 30).

The year of their liberation proved but a continuation of the Moodies' "untoward destiny" in certain ways. Two losses were particularly emotional and difficult to bear. First, on 8 August, their sixth child, George Arthur, died less than a month after his birth. Conceived in the backwoods just before John departed for Belleville, he was named for the man who had done so much to help them. Ironically, given the rough conditions of many of her previous confinements, he was the first child Susanna lost. Then, in December, they were "burnt out" of their first Belleville house, a fate they had managed to avoid, despite several near disasters, in the backwoods. For a time during the fire, Susanna was terrified that Johnny, her youngest, was lost, and the anxiety she had felt as a result of earlier fires she had experienced was powerfully revisited upon her. Relatedly, the Moodies' struggle to regain control of their meagre finances suffered a further jolt from this "great calamity" (*Life* 13).

At the same time, John Moodie's life as a sheriff was quickly proving a greater test than he had anticipated. Writing to Susanna in November 1839, he had shrewdly assessed the dangerous aspects of the situation he faced: "Parties, as usual, run high here, and [I] find some difficulty in steering a middle course, which I am determined to do. I now see my way pretty clearly, and I shall have less trouble (I expect) than in my last year's employment" (*Letters* 159). In the same letter, however, he also noted three other factors that, considered from the perspective of later events, did not bode well. First, many prominent citizens were trying to draw him into the quagmire of "miserable petty party and national feeling" that characterized Belleville (161). His strategy was to remain uncommitted and detached, to be a kind of mediator rather than a participant:

> The two Doctors Ridley & Marshall both tollerably [sic] well disposed men on other points are the two opposite extremes in this way, and both are ready to give and take offence on every occasion. I am labouring to smooth the mutual prejudices of these differing Doctors, — . I go to both Churches, and most of my countrymen go to the English Church when Mr. Ketcham [the Presbyterian minister] is absent. The Episcopalians, however, are not liberal enough to follow this laudable *example*. (161)

Second, because of his parachute appointment, Moodie found himself a designated enemy of many prominent Belleville tories. He was an outsider and was made to feel it. In particular, Thomas Parker, a former postmaster who had coveted the shrievalty, in a flamboyant gesture of protest to Moodie's appointment, had resigned his position as magistrate in the town. Doubtless, Sir George Arthur made matters worse by simply accepting Parker's resignation. According to Moodie, Parker was "half crazy" in his "disappointment," and "like to bite the ends of his fingers off" when his resignation was accepted (161). Parker would soon focus his energies on undermining John Moodie's position.

Third, despite his conscious attempt to keep a middle ground in Belleville's political jungle, Moodie was the subject of criticism by at least one prominent local newspaper even before he officially took office. By way of attacking his appointment, Doctor Edward John Barker of the Kingston *Whig* had labelled him a dangerous reformer, "an out and out advocate of *Responsible Gov*ᵗ" (161). Such an indictment seems ridiculous today, but it carried great weight among Belleville's leading conservatives. Such a charge, however, seemed to Moodie a nuisance he could overcome in due time by pursuing a careful middle course.

One of Susanna Moodie's most telling comments in *Roughing It in the Bush* occurs in response to news of the 1837 Rebellion: "The honest backwoodsmen, perfectly ignorant of the abuses that had led to the present position of things, regarded the rebels as a set of monsters, for whom no punishment was too severe, and obeyed the call to arms with enthusiasm" (413). Susanna and her husband saw themselves as just such "honest backwoodsmen"; hence, while John rushed off to make his military contribution, she wrote inflammatory and patriotic poems, wishing failure if not death to Mackenzie and his fellow rebels. Soon enough, however, John came to see things differently. His military experience and travel in 1838-39 made him aware that there were legitimate grounds for unrest among the general populace of Upper Canada; he saw the need for an intelligent approach to change in order to forestall increased internal unrest and growing pro-American sympathy. Viewing himself as a moderate, he was committed to nonviolent and progressive reform within the British system; he could support neither the cause of "Revolutionary Radicalism," such as he associated with Mackenzie, nor the "ultra selfish Toryism," an outlook that for him characterized the politics of the Family Compact (*Letters* 150).

When John Moodie read the substance of Lord Durham's report in a newspaper in the spring of 1839, he found himself in general agreement with the changes suggested there. Here was a ray of hope. "A black cloud hangs over Canada," he wrote to Susanna on 24 May 1839:

> It may pass away and bright sunshine succeed, — but if it breaks, God help this wretched country. I wish I could think more cheerfully on this subject. Lord Durham's report has stirred up a hornet's nest. Hardly any one can talk or think cooly about it. I believe the middle course is the only safe one in this case, as in many others. It contains a great many home truths — and it is these truths which have given offence. . . . If the British Gov^t has the discernment to adopt his suggestions on some very important points it is my firm belief that he will yet be regarded as the best friend Canada ever had. (*Letters* 151)

Among those "very important points" was the need for some kind of responsible government in the Canadas. For her part, once Susanna understood the abuses practised by the tories, she readily agreed with her husband's view of the country's most pressing needs. They were in fact of one mind in most of their political thinking. And certainly Dr. Barker had pegged Moodie's reformist sympathies correctly in the tory-ish Kingston *Whig*. The problem was that what John Moodie considered to be a middle ground was anathema to the conservatives in Kingston and Belleville. They aggressively labelled such thinking as both radical and disloyal, and they sought opportunities to harass him, to undermine his actions as sheriff, and to hamper the collection of fees upon which his income depended.

The matter of obtaining his sureties proved a case in point.

Drawing upon his Douro connections, Moodie enlisted support from Sam Strickland and Thomas A. Stewart. He was, however, turned down by a conservative Belleville magistrate on the grounds that Strickland was not known to him. Moodie then turned to two men whom he had befriended during his militia work, Sheldon Hawley and Adam Henry Meyers of River Trent (now Trenton); though both were conservatives, they were sufficiently distanced from Belleville biases to offer Moodie their support. Despite the approval of these sureties in Belleville, Moodie's problems with the town's powerful coterie of conservative lawyers and magistrates were just beginning. They would continue in one form or another during his twenty-three years as sheriff, culminating in a lawsuit that cost him his position in 1863. In the short run, by means of vexatious suits and refusals to pay sums owed to him, the tory lawyers made his work as difficult as they could manage within the boundaries of established law and local practice.

There is a tendency among Canadian literary critics to ignore or dismiss John Moodie as if somehow he constituted an embarrassment in the otherwise interesting study of his wife as writer and personality. To do so, however, is to overlook both his competence and the intimacy that characterized their marriage. It is also to ignore the extent to which Susanna's politicized views were rooted in the experiences they shared. Indeed, in John's attempt to fashion a middle way, to sail between the archconservatism of Family Compact self-interest and the radical reform associated with William Lyon Mackenzie's republicanism, the Moodies, drawing on their Scottish and English heritages and their liberal-leaning values, together forged and advocated an approach that in retrospect is suggestive of the kind of thinking that Canada itself developed. In his idealistic and often naïve way, John took the lead in that development.

That his approach proved costly and problematic during his career as sheriff in no sense diminishes its significance; neither does it diminish the value that both he and Susanna found in it. Rather, it should remind us that the outlook they valued and persisted in was fraught with pitfalls and opposition as well as its own contradictions.

While John carried on as sheriff and Susanna chafed at the unfairness of the treatment he was receiving, she devoted much of her newly gained leisure to writing for John Lovell's *Literary Garland.* As her health and energy had improved in her final months in the backwoods, she had managed to send Lovell a few stories in the summer and fall of 1839, but it was in 1840 that she became a regular contributor and began to reap the monetary advantages of the offer he had made to her. Lovell, whom she called "a most liberal and kind friend," paid her "five pounds per sheet" while allowing her to keep the copyright of all he published for future use (*Susanna Moodie* 99). Her first serialized novel — "Geoffrey Moncton" — appeared in nine instalments from December 1839 to August 1840. Virtually every year until December 1851, when the magazine ceased publication, she managed to supply a similar serial — "The First Debt: A Tale of Every Day" (1841), "The Miser and His Son," later *Mark Hurdlestone* (1842), and "Mildred Rosier: A Tale of the Ruined City" (1844) are early examples. In off-years, there were shorter serials, and always there were poems and short sketches or stories (many of which had been published a decade earlier in London, either on her own accord or with the help of her sisters).

One of her few surviving letters to Lovell (26 November 1842) makes clear the warm friendship Susanna developed with him. In that letter, while sharing details of her family life and concerns, she tendered her account for the year at "forty pounds, ten shillings," eighty percent of which was for prose contributions. She also thanked him for the safe delivery of a piano, which he had purchased for her and arranged to have sent from Montreal. She was to pay for it through her current and future earnings. Although she was pregnant at the time — "life on these occasions is very uncertain, especially with me," she told him — she also spoke of her growing literary ambitions. She had been "in treaty for the copy right" of "Geoffrey Moncton" and "Mark Hurdlestone" with Harper and Brothers in New York, though she had "not heard from them since their great loss by fire," and she hoped to send a letter of inquiry about publishing possibilities to her husband's London publisher, Richard Bentley, if she could find the time (*Susanna Moodie* 97). While the Harper connection did not materialize and her plan to contact Bentley remained but an idea for years, Susanna continued to be Lovell's literary lioness, rivalling only Elizabeth L. Cushing in the regularity of her appearances.

### ELECTIONS, PARTY JOURNALISM, AND RACISM IN BELLEVILLE

John Moodie's public life took a violent turn with the first election in the united Canadas. As sheriff of Hastings County, it was his duty to serve as the returning officer for the election, and in Belleville, where his reformist sympathies had been clearly identified, the contest became particularly heated. A local lawyer named Edmund Murney was the conservative incumbent. He was not only prominent in Belleville society and a near neighbour of the Moodies but also, according to contemporary reports, a consistent tory of the extreme kind. The election was a kind of litmus test of the new order — a measuring of the effects of the Durham-directed reform of the system and the capacity of the Upper Canadian reformers, led by Robert Baldwin, to set a new agenda for the colony. But also at issue, and so positioned to obscure the real concerns of the reformist agenda, was the emotional question of loyalty to Britain. Susanna defined the problem succinctly and bitterly in *Life in the Clearings*:

> The Tory party, who arrogated the whole loyalty of the colony to themselves, branded, indiscriminately, the large body of Reformers as traitors and rebels. Every conscientious and thinking man who wished to see a change for the better in the management of public affairs was confounded with those discontented spirits who had raised the standard of revolt against the mother country. In justice even to them, it must be said, not without severe provocation; and their disaffection was more towards the colonial government, and the abuses it fostered, than any particular dislike to British supremacy or institutions. . . . (35)

A fervent British patriot herself, she was deeply angered by the unfairness of such a charge. She was as committed as her husband to the cause of reform, but she could only stand by while he was subjected to numerous, often ad hominem attacks in the local tory newspaper, George Benjamin's Belleville *Intelligencer*.

The first election took place in March-April 1841. The Belleville area quickly became a focal point of provincial attention when Robert Baldwin, who had just been appointed solicitor-general of Canada West (Upper Canada), decided to test the tory strength in Belleville by running against Murney. Already assured of election in the fourth riding of York, Baldwin (who could legally run in several ridings) plunged the tories into heated concern. His presence and attractiveness as a candidate made them desperate, for he had the capacity to draw together the many factions in the surrounding area that were not conservative in their

Robert Baldwin.

thinking. It also increased the level of name-calling and media-orchestrated hostility. Although Baldwin was actually Murney's cousin by marriage, there was no love lost between the candidates. Murney's platform antics shocked Moodie; Murney labelled Baldwin a rebel, a papist, and an outsider, using every possible means to undermine his opponent's integrity without addressing the major issues at stake. Moodie had no doubt that the tories would align themselves with the Orange Order if necessary, and he knew that the local Orangemen were spoiling for a fight. At the election itself, which took place on two dates and in two locales, Returning Officer Moodie worriedly oversaw the voting, fearful that serious violence would erupt.

When Baldwin narrowly won the vote, the local tories immediately began a program of invective against John Moodie and the local reformers. Thomas Parker launched a formal appeal of the election results, the aim of which seemed to be both to discredit the result and the returning officer. Within a year, however, another provincial election was required, and the same contestants squared off again. This time violence did break out at the hustings, aided by Orange Order support for Murney. Months earlier, in fact, a concerned John Moodie had sought to initiate a petition in the Legislative Assembly to ban the legality of such dangerous secret societies. In the second election, with some injuries reported and both sides armed, the sheriff felt he had no choice but to call in the troops and shut down the voting in the interest of public safety. Again he was much maligned by the Belleville *Intelligencer* and other conservative papers, both for the biased way in which he was seen to conduct the election and for his decision to close the polls. Murney was leading at the time, and the action was interpreted as a last-minute manoeuvre to prevent his victory. When Moodie declared the voting process sufficiently flawed to render a nondecision (Murney himself had signed a paper at the hustings agreeing that there had been serious voting irregularities), he was praised by reformers and further vilified by tories. In the aftermath of the debacle, however, another tory-initiated petition resulted in Moodie's being relieved of his returning-officer duties. Murney was awarded the victory, and Baldwin, realizing the dangers of continuing to force the issue in the charged Belleville arena, wisely withdrew himself from further direct involvement in Hastings County.

John Moodie's exposure to Belleville politics was a chastening one. Doubtless he was relieved to step aside and confine himself to the shrievalty. If anything, however, the tory lawyers and judges stepped up their campaign of harassment against him. In the aftermath of the second election, his conservative sureties, Hawley and Meyers, were convinced to withdraw their support, and he was again forced to dispute with the local magistrate about the worth of the replacements he brought forward. Nuisance suits and strategies for reducing the fees to which he was entitled continued to cut into his earnings, for his remuneration depended on his activities as sheriff, not on a set salary. Much disturbed by such activities, Moodie argued, in letters to Robert Baldwin in 1845, that sheriffs in the province ought to be paid a regular salary rather than be required to make their living by collecting fines and charging fees for services (*Letters* 193-97).

Such concerns may seem at first glance somewhat off-centre in a biography of Susanna Moodie. The reason is, however, evident — the problems John faced in his professional and public life affected her deeply, chafing her sense of unfairness and arousing her desire to defend her husband and to exact some revenge on his enemies. That desire soon found voice in her writing. Although no copies of the Belleville *Intelligencer* exist for this divisive period, we know that George Benjamin, its founder and editor, was a die-hard

conservative and Orangeman who regularly attacked and
disparaged John Moodie in his various roles as sheriff,
returning officer, and public figure. Articles picked up from
the *Intelligencer* and reprinted in other tory papers in Canada
West give a flavour of his work. But Benjamin himself had a
not-so-well-kept secret — though he presented himself as an
Englishman and an Orangeman, he was an English Jew who
had arrived in Belleville in the early 1830s and disguised his
background as best he could. In fact, his Orange Order
activities led to his election in 1846 as grand master of the
Orange Order for British North America.

Goaded by Benjamin's partisan attacks in the *Intelligencer*,
Susanna took up her pen for battle. In her story "Richard
Redpath, the Voluntary Slave," she included a figure named
Benjamin Levi, the villainous editor of the *Jamaica Observer*,
"a violent party paper, which most strenuously opposed the
abolition of the slave trade, and denounced the few benevolent men who set their faces against the abhorred trade . . .
as traitors to Great Britain and enemies of their country"
(qtd. in *Susanna Moodie* 88). Mixing caricaturish humour
with fact (Levi, like Benjamin, founds his own paper, revels
in notoriety, and disguises his Jewishness), she made good
her project of literary revenge. Replacing Benjamin's Upper
Canadian conservatism with a proslavery program not out
of place in English-language newspapers in the Caribbean of
the time, she maintained her liberal and progressive point
of view, bolstered no doubt by her own earlier involvement
in antislavery writing. That she indulged in anti-Semitism in
reviling the tactics and ethics of her *"Jew Editor"* did not
seem to trouble her. A decade later (January 1854), she told
Richard Bentley that Levi was "a true picture drawn from
life, which so closely resembles the original, that it will be
recognized by all who ever knew him, or fell under his lash.
A man *detested* in his day and generation" (*Susanna Moodie*

George Benjamin, 1859.

147). Having felt that lash, she felt fully justified in seeking retribution. While Moodie could deplore the "prejudice against race and colour" as "a dreadful thing" (*Life*, 26), she drew readily and with some apparent satisfaction on the stock and trade of anti-Semitism.

The story appeared as a short serial in 1843 in the *Literary Garland* and the *Toronto Star*, and later as part of her book *Matrimonial Speculations* (1854). The strategy was deeply rooted in the biases and assumptions of Moodie's time and place. The narrative served at once as a thinly veiled denunciation of party politics and biased journalism in Upper Canada and as her personal revenge on Benjamin; using the language of satire and parody, Susanna set out to counter the language of his partisan and ad hominem attacks in the *Intelligencer*. Her grievances, in her mind, legitimately overrode any errors her husband may have made in his various public activities. She was, she felt, just as correct in deploring the evils of slavery as she was in celebrating the virtues of responsible government. Nevertheless, as in *Roughing It in the Bush*, she tried to use humour — her own irrepressible sense of the comic and mischievous — to temper the raw edges of her vindictiveness. On one level, her Benjamin Levi is much like her portraits of Uncle Joe Harris and Old Satan: "I don't know what we should do without Benjamin Levi," says one of her female characters in the story, apropos the humorous aspects of his villainy — "he keeps us alive" (qtd. in *Susanna Moodie* 89).

## SETTLING IN AND MAKING A CAREER

By 1843, the most public of John Moodie's misadventures as sheriff and returning officer were over. Still, the Moodies' commitment to what Robert Baldwin represented for Canada's future remained strong. The pregnancy that Susanna alluded to in her 1842 letter to John Lovell resulted in the birth, on 8 July 1843, of her fourth surviving son, whom they duly named Robert Baldwin Moodie in honour of their friend. John Moodie later shared with Baldwin a favourite family story. "[W]hen the Chief Justice [John Beverly Robinson] called upon us during the Assizes here, [he] overhear[d] some remarks we were making as to the effect *that dreaded name* might produce on his *conservative nerves*. . . ." Intrigued but puzzled by the comments, Robinson innocently asked Moodie's son Johnny the name of the baby. The boy slyly replied, "we *sometimes* call him *Robert*" (*Letters* 195).

Much chastened by the continuing daily hassles he faced, John Moodie began to seek other means of improving his income and situation. Writing to Robert Baldwin on 6 February 1845, he articulated his desire for a less political position and his need for a steadier and better income:

> For some time back I have carefully abstained from taking any part whatever in politics and did not even vote at the last election. While I still feel as strongly as I always did towards the great principle of Responsible Government . . . [I must look after myself]. I have no doubt my conduct will be misrepresented to you on this head, but at the age of nearly 50 with a large family entirely dependant on the paltry office I hold for bread, and unable to cloth[e] them as well as respectable mechanics can do — I think you can hardly blame me if I endeavour *at last* to take some care of myself.
> (*Letters* 193-94)

If one detects a sense of weariness here, it owes at least as much to a family tragedy as to John's problems with the Belleville conservatives. That tragedy was the drowning of five-year-old Johnny in the Moira River in the spring of 1844.

Having gone fishing with his older brothers, he apparently came home alone to show his mother a specimen he had caught. En route, he slipped off a dock and drowned in the turbulence of the spring runoff.

To read Susanna's letters to John in 1839 is to sense how much this child of her harrowing final winter in the backwoods meant to her. Margaret Atwood accurately touched that nerve in her powerful poem "Death of a Young Son by Drowning." The last two stanzas read:

> After the long trip I was tired of waves.
> My foot hit rock. The dreamed sails
> collapsed, ragged.
>
> I planted him in this country
> like a flag. (31)

Susanna Moodie reached a new level of despair with that loss. Her "fine talented boy" to whom "her soul clave" was the source of tremendous grief, of "agony unspeakable," and the subject of two poems, "The Mother's Lament" and "The Early Lost." In the former, she confessed that "all my past sorrows were nothing to this" (*Life* 27); in the latter, she feared that "The voice of mirth is silenced in my heart" (28). A new wave of religious uncertainty — "The hand of God has press'd me very sore," she wrote (28) — may have contributed to the Moodies' brief flirtation with a small Congregational church in Belleville in 1844, a flirtation that led from membership to their "ex-communication" several months later for what the church leaders termed "disorderly walk."

In the long run, Susanna Moodie recovered something of her spontaneity and mirth. Out of her grievous loss, her sense of life's mixed blessings deepened and her perceptions of her own fate grew more complex. What became implicit for her is made explicit in Atwood's evocative poem. In planting Johnny "like a flag" in Canadian soil, Susanna committed herself more fully to her life in the New World. The rest of the 1840s passed with less disruption and pain. Settling into a more comfortable life in Belleville, Susanna was largely absorbed in her family's needs and the education of her children. While no close female friend seems to have emerged for her during these years, there were many social opportunities and connections to be developed. For Lovell, she wrote and copied steadily even as she explored other literary possibilities. Having to reconcile her bluestockings with a society that, like Cobourg, undervalued literary and imaginative expression, she tried to be as unliterary as possible in public. While John gave occasional lectures at the Mechanics Institute, she wrote in privacy.

Where possible, Susanna helped her struggling sister Catharine, particularly in connecting her with John Lovell, whose generous terms provided some much-needed income. She visited Catharine when she could, and as the years went by, she took various of her sister's children into her house for extended periods of time. James Traill and his younger sister Mary became particularly close and devoted to their aunt. Her interest in supporting and helping to develop literary culture in Canada increased as she recovered from the devastating loss of her son. Writing an encouraging letter to a promising author named Louisa May Murray (13 January 1851), Susanna noted the "low esteem in which all literary labor is held in this country" and offered to help her as much as she could in her "literary career" (*Susanna Moodie* 99). Indeed, the more she became established as one of Lovell's major contributors, the more she sought to encourage other writers, be they younger or older.

The venture that most typifies her encouragement and

fostering of other voices was the *Victoria Magazine*, a non-partisan monthly that she and John edited for a year in Belleville for Joseph Wilson. Designed as "a cheap periodical" or inexpensive magazine to distinguish it from Lovell's well-established, tonier enterprise, it was aimed at the industrious yeomen and mechanics who were, to the Moodies, the real future of Canada. As they noted in the August 1848 issue, they hoped to do their part as "literary philanthropists" in contributing to "the exalted and noble cause of mental improvement" in a country where book publication was limited and lending libraries were lacking (288). While the magazine became a convenient vehicle for their own writing, they included as many "Canadian" writers as they could make contact with. In addition to providing an outlet for authors such as Rhoda Ann Page (R.A.P.), Thomas Page, Hamilton Aylmer, Thomas MacQueen, and James McCarroll, they planned to introduce Louisa May Murray's "Fauna, the Red Flower of Leafy Hollow," which she had submitted to them in the summer of 1848. Financial constraints, however, closed the publication before that promising story could appear. It appears that not enough yeomen and mechanics were prepared to subscribe to the magazine to carry it beyond its first year.

The *Victoria Magazine* also provided an outlet for Strickland relatives. The now famous Agnes Strickland, who had once suggested that Susanna and Catharine might start a magazine in Upper Canada, provided several poems and sketches. Although her subject matter was English, her name was an attraction on which the Moodies felt they could rely. From Douro, Sam Strickland (who cast himself as "Pioneer") contributed sketches about settlement life, and from Rice Lake, Catharine Parr Traill sent in a few pieces, though her domestic circumstances were so constrained that she had little time for writing at that point. Significantly, from Susanna's point of view, the magazine was an important part of the incubation of the writing project that became *Roughing It in the Bush* (288).

Susanna was deeply engaged in autobiographical writing at the time she was editing the magazine. While several sketches for what would become *Roughing It in the Bush* appeared in the *Literary Garland* in 1847, she also published what would be that book's first two sketches, "A Visit to Grosse Isle" and "First Impressions. Quebec," in the *Victoria Magazine* in the September and November 1847 under the general title "Scenes in Canada." As the magazine's first-published or signature piece, she chose her celebratory poem "Canada," in which she praised the country as "the bless'd — the free" and envisioned the "glory" of its future "page" in "the world's great story" (3). She also included her essay on making dandelion coffee in the September 1847 issue. Out of the same self-reflective impulse, she published — beginning in January 1848 — the seven parts of her romantic reading of her early life under the title "Rachel Wilde; or Trifles from the Burthen of a Life."

Clearly, the period 1846-48 was crucial for Moodie as a writer. Little that she wrote would be of so much interest in Canada today if she had not so fully given herself to the retrospective and deeply personal impulse that seized her in these years. Why did she do so? And why at that time? The root of the answer to the first question lies in the fact that she was a highly self-absorbed writer from the beginning. That self-absorption is particularly evident in many of her early poems, a few of her sketches, and her surviving letters. But it became a particularly powerful force during these years.

What Susanna needed was a set of personal experiences compelling enough to force her to break free of the narrative conventions on which she usually relied. By 1847, she was forty-four years old and seven years removed from the cauldron of the backwoods, from that riveting set of adventures and tests that she would tellingly label "this great epoch in our lives" (*Roughing* 196). Those years had altered, tried, and aged her. As well, they led her to ruminate more deeply about herself and her life, and they triggered in her a desire to record them and give them a shape. Once in Belleville, she could begin to apply a perspective to those experiences. At the same time, the escape of Belleville provided a closure on what must have often seemed a set of random and daunting events. It is impossible, of course, to measure the effect of young Johnny's death in this equation, but I would speculate that it was no small factor in tipping Susanna into writing so personally and feelingly about the cards that her life in Canada had dealt her.

Coincidentally, there was a surprising drop-off in Moodie's contributions to the *Literary Garland* in 1849 and 1850. Only two poems appeared there during those two years. Since there are no surviving letters to account for this hiatus, we must cast about for plausible explanations.

The first was Susanna's need for a less demanding schedule after her long run as a serial writer and her efforts as an editor in 1847-48. That said, it is evident that the period of 1849-50 was busy and creative for Moodie. What appears limited in terms of published output was in fact aesthetically rich. Arguably, it was part of the richest period of creativity she would ever know. She devoted much of her writing time to the task of revising her 1847-48 sketches and developing a good deal of new material about the backwoods. The manuscript, as she expanded it, also included as its natural starting point the narrative that detailed the Moodies' preparations to emigrate and their travels via Edinburgh to Canada. In fact, that story made a second book.

As Susanna described the process, she "took a freak of

cutting it out of the MS," thus choosing to begin the manuscript with their arrival at the Canadian point of entry, Grosse Isle. Taking "a freak" sounds rather impulsive and accidental. It can, however, be read more positively, as in "made an intuitive artistic decision." Certainly, her creative judgement was the right one, for it had several benefits. In separating the early part of the emigration story from the manuscript, Susanna made the experience of Canada the major focus of *Roughing It in the Bush*. She gave the narrative a shape she could work with; she could play her two separate settlements off against one another, giving each a volume of its own and thereby enhancing the range and authority of her presentation. The remainder of the manuscript, clearly material of less force, she kept separate, calling it "Trifles from the Burthen of a Life" (the second time in a few years that she had assigned that title to a manuscript of her autobiographical writing). Always alert to dollars, she sent it to John Lovell, who published it in five sections in the *Literary Garland* in 1851, and later she used it as the basis for her lightly fictionalized novel *Flora Lyndsay* (1854). Clearly, then, the autobiographical impulse, so strong in 1847-48, had not died. It was during 1849-50 that her autobiographical energy was most fully and productively focused.

Not to be forgotten during those years were the upbringing and educational needs of Moodie's children. By 1849, Katie was eighteen, the beautiful Agnes sixteen, and Dunbar fifteen. Donald, in whom Susanna (especially after the death of Johnny) placed so much concern and invested so much hope of success, was thirteen, and Robert six. Agnes was married the following summer, on 21 August. The marriage was a social event of considerable Upper Canadian significance, for, beyond the literary fame of her parents, Agnes's husband was a young Toronto barrister, Charles Thomas Fitzgibbon, one of the sons of the famous colonel James

Fitzgibbon, who had distinguished himself in the War of
1812 and again in the Rebellion of 1837.

## THE FRUSTRATING FIFTIES

In terms of books published — there were six — the 1850s
were by far Susanna Moodie's most productive and impres-
sive decade. That output, however, is very misleading. It
belies the creative energy she poured into her writing in the
1840s, when most of what went into those books was actually
written. The 1850s were, in fact, more a period of copying
and expanding, of juggling British and American publishing
opportunities as they came to her, and of feeling the heavy
cost of public notoriety in ways that she had never before
experienced. Such, finally, was her dismay and creative
exhaustion that, by decade's end, her writing career was
virtually over. With the exception of the sketches about
Upper Canadian life that she wrote hurriedly for *Life in the
Clearings versus the Bush* in 1852-53, very little that was new
came from her pen in this decade. It was as if the surge of
autobiographical commitment that produced the three books
of emigration and settlement — *Flora Lyndsay*, *Roughing It
in the Bush*, and *Life in the Clearings versus the Bush* —
brought to an end her creative energies as a writer. Her other
products of the 1850s and 1860s reflect a formulaic sameness
that pales in comparison to the vitality of her personal narratives.

*Roughing It in the Bush* appeared in London in February
1852. Working first through her husband's old friend and
fellow Scot, John Bruce, Susanna sent him a manuscript that
was bolstered and made more authoritative for settlers by
contributions from John and Sam Strickland. When "Michael
Macbride" provoked the ire of Irish Catholics and in particular the editor of the *True Witness and Catholic Chronicle*

(Montreal) on its appearance in the *Literary Garland* in January 1851, she chose to withdraw it from the Bentley manuscript. What she sent in its place and in response to Bruce's request for more material arrived too late for inclusion in the book — thus, "Jeanie Burns" and "Lost Children" could not be included, though John's long, dull essay, unhelpfully entitled "Canadian Sketches," was added to the second edition (also in 1852) because its inclusion at the end of volume 2 involved no change in structure or pagination.

*Roughing It in the Bush* was an immediate success in London, drawing largely rave reviews in influential literary papers such as the *Athenaeum*, the *Spectator*, the *Literary Gazette*, and *Blackwood's*. The solitary sour note was offered by the *Observer*, (15 February 1852) which objected to the treatment of the Irish in the book. According to that paper, Moodie described Irish emigrants "in terms which a reflective writer would scarcely apply to a pack of hounds"; its reviewer further chastised Moodie for overlooking the fact that "it was to the kindness, the charity, and the disinterested services of poor Irish emigrants and settlers that she and her family were indebted for, perhaps the only real benevolence she had encountered in Canada" (qtd. in *Susanna Moodie* 108). That review, reprinted in the Montreal *Pilot* (27 March 1852), added to Moodie's anxiety about the Irish reaction. Still smarting from the accusations of the *True Witness and Catholic Chronicle* a year earlier (she had been seen there as an English "lady" who was "evidently ignorant of all the genuine characteristics of that fine people" and as a Protestant with no knowledge of the depth of Catholic faith), she felt the sting deeply (qtd. in *Susanna Moodie* 109). To her mind, she had been meanly accused of *"hatred to the Irish,"* which, she assured John Lovell, was not at all the case. Acutely sensitive to and resentful of the political machinations of Canadian newspaper editors after her decade in

Belleville, she objected to being made a pawn in English-Irish hostility and to being held up to the public in so volatile a way. The mood in Canada was such that she could imagine her "home stead" being "burnt over my head" in angry Irish response. Everything she had written was based on fact, she insisted; she had written nothing as critical of the Irish as what Charles Lever, himself an Irishman, had included in his novel *Con-Cregan, the Irish Gil Blas: His Confessions and Experiences* (see *Letters* 218).

Within months of its English publication, *Roughing It in the Bush* was readily available in North America. Taking advantage of copyright loopholes, New York publisher George P. Putnam hurried out an American edition in June 1852, slightly modified to suit American tastes by its editor, Charles Franco Briggs. As a result, the book was reviewed in numerous Canadian and American papers. Most of the latter were highly complimentary. However, several of the Canadian reviews (some of which have not survived) were critical of the book, and those reactions bothered Moodie deeply.

It is not clear what she expected of Canadian reviewers. She had, as we have seen, little faith in the capacity of Canadian journalists to be nonpolitical, temperate, or even-handed. Likely, she had neither carefully considered how the book might be read by certain groups in Canada nor accurately gauged the extent of her literary power. She had a variety of stories to tell in the book. One of them, read from the point of view of businessmen interested in developing the country and promoting it to potential emigrants, was a complaint that required an answer, if not a forceful rebuttal. What was ostensibly a book written to warn members of the British middle class and gentry about the losses involved in trying to settle in the backwoods of Canada in fact delivered a complex set of messages. Despite her complaints and warnings, Moodie also strove to depict herself as one who believed in Canada's future and welcomed the opportunities the country presented to those in search of an independent life.

The book's blanketlike alternate title *Life in Canada*, however, opened the narrative up to indictments based on opposing interpretations and selective citation in their responses. In the *Examiner* (Toronto), on 16 June 1852, for instance, Charles Lindsey, under the title "Misrepresentation," attacked *Roughing It in the Bush* without naming either the author or the book. Taking exception to the positive review Moodie's book had received in *Blackwood's*, Lindsay sought to make the case for Canada as a settled, productive, and advancing country, not a wilderness. "The diffusion of sound information respecting the condition and resources of the country is a matter which could not fail to tell very powerfully on its material progress as well as on the social prosperity of the people" (qtd. in Thompson 204). Viewing *Roughing It in the Bush* as "simply a novel" and "a most mischievous one, moreover," founded on the "experience of a disappointed settler" (203), Lindsay described its author as "an ape of the aristocracy, too poor to lie on a sofa and too proud to labour for a living" (203). Susanna could laugh at that depiction of herself, especially when Lindsay apologized a year later. The editor of the *United Empire*, who gave the book what she regarded as its worst review, also later apologized to her, telling her in a private letter that he hadn't actually read the book when he wrote his response.

The defenders of Irish character and Canadian business interests were not the only ones who succeeded in getting beneath Susanna Moodie's thin skin. Even more galling in personal terms was the reaction of her sister Agnes, to whom, with an astute eye for marketing, Susanna had dedicated *Roughing It in the Bush*. Agnes apparently took a strong objection to being associated with a book about vulgar people, and in her outrage she ordered her sister to drop her name from it. When Richard Bentley complied with Agnes's request, Susanna thanked him in terms that make clear her pain: "She has wounded my feelings so severely about this dedication, that it is to me a perfect eye sore in front of my unfortunate book. Could I have foreseen her reception of it, thousands would not have induced me to place it there" (*Susanna Moodie* 136). Years later, another sister, the widowed Sarah, would recall the indignation at Reydon Hall that followed the appearance of the book. It was as if Susanna had descended to the depths and wanted to drag Agnes and the Strickland family down among the vulgar with her (Patrick Hamilton Ewing Collection, Sarah Gwillym to Katie Vickers, Nov. 1874).

Thus, while *Roughing It in the Bush* made Susanna Moodie an international celebrity, she was deeply bruised by various reactions, so bruised in fact that, by the fall of 1853, she told Bentley that with "Flora Lyndsay" she had written her last book on Canada: "I am sick of the subject, and it awakens ill feelings in others" (*Susanna Moodie* 135). A few months later, in April 1854, she told her sister Catharine, "I never mean to write for Canadian paper or magazine again, after their unjust abuse of me" (152).

Even before *Roughing It in the Bush* made its éclat, Susanna was hard at work expanding and copying her story, "Mark Hurdlestone, the Gold Worshipper," in the hope that Bentley might take it. With John Bruce too ill to continue to represent her interests, she wrote directly to the publisher, thus laying the groundwork for what must have been one of her most important and satisfying literary correspondences. Her plan, as she explained it to Bentley, was to offer a series of tales such as had enjoyed "very great popularity" in the *Literary Garland* (*Susanna Moodie* 123); they "might aptly enough be styled 'Tales of a Canadian Winter Hearth,'" she told him, "although the scenes and characters described are not Canadian" (124). Bentley speedily complied, and *Mark Hurdlestone* was published in 1853. His real desire, however, was to have Moodie write a sequel to *Roughing It in the Bush.* By the time Bentley's formal request reached Susanna in Canada, she was doubly incapacitated. She had been "suffering much from ill health lately" and was angrily nursing her sense of injustice concerning public reaction in Canada to *Roughing It in the Bush.* Nowhere is her vulnerability and naïveté more evident than in her response to Bentley's idea. She wished to distance herself from the "natives" in the land she called her new home:

> I will think over the new Canadian work, but the little that I have said of Canadian society has made me so unpopular with the natives, that I believe it would be better to leave them alone for the future, if I would hope to live in peace. Yet I have said nothing of them beyond the truth, nor told half of what could, and ought to be said, of their unfaithful dealings, and utter disregard of all honorable feeling. (*Susanna Moodie* 127)

The ill health to which Susanna alluded in her letter of 20 July 1852 not only temporarily curtailed her writing but soon proved life-threatening. Serious haemorrhaging confined her to bed for much of the summer and left her in a weakened state. A recuperatory boat trip to Toronto (to visit her daughter Agnes and her children) and to Niagara Falls was the recommendation of her vigilant Belleville doctors. That holiday proved salutary in two ways; it refreshed her emotionally and provided her with a new literary subject. For the first time since she had arrived in the colony in 1832, she was able to travel extensively in Canada West (Upper Canada) and think about its development.

Back in Belleville, Susanna suffered another distressful

Richard Bentley, c. 1860.

AN ENGRAVING BY JOSEPH BROWN FROM A PHOTOGRAPH BY LOCK AND
WHITFIELD OF LONDON. BY PERMISSION OF THE BRITISH LIBRARY (R98/1391).

haemorrhage in late autumn. Having "looked upon Death face to face, as it were," she reported to Bentley from her bedroom that she was much weakened and "a sort of living skeleton" but was on the mend.

My case it appears, has been a very singular one, and nature has thrown off without the aid of [the doctors'] dreadful knives, one of those painful internal complaints which are generally fatal to all attacked by them, and which was the cause of my long and obstinate illness during the whole of last summer. (*Susanna Moodie* 128)

Much revived in spirits, she was ready to take "great pleasure" (128) in writing a book about "the *present state of Canada*" that would "form a sort of apendix [sic] to *Roughing It in the Bush*" (129; for more on Moodie's illness, see *Letters* 267).

*Life in the Clearings versus the Bush* appeared in 1853. Much more than *Roughing It in the Bush*, it is a cobbled affair, a work of hasty application and construction. The limits of Moodie's Canadian experience and the resultant thinness of her material are lightly masked by the inclusion of the sketches that had arrived too late for *Roughing It in the Bush* and various narratives Moodie had at hand. That said, it is an important book that blends many fresh, on-the-scene observations of Upper Canadian life with Moodie's attempt not only to justify the contents of *Roughing It in the Bush* but also to clarify her views about Canada's problems and the sources of its future greatness. Although she often self-consciously undercut her ability to write with authority about larger issues (the historical, political, and statistical) on the ground that women were better suited to observe and comment on smaller, everyday things, *Life in the Clearings versus the Bush* reveals her willingness to risk engaging again in the (treacherous) debate about Canada and her ability to assert her own views with forcefulness and humour. Those elements in her arguments that now seem contradictory and even muddled were rooted in the very nature of her Canadian experience, in the commitment she shared with her husband to articulate a viable and morally tenable position amid the cacophony of racial, religious, political, and class-based ideologies that vied for attention and power of Upper Canada. At once aggressive and shrinking, judgemental and forgiving, cultural commentator and fastidious gentlewoman, she could not resist the opportunity to have her say again, even as a side of herself counselled silence. Neither could she avoid the consequences of revealing a good deal of herself in the process.

By the end of 1853, it was clear that, in Britain at least, neither *Mark Hurdlestone* nor *Life in the Clearings versus the Bush* had been a successful follow-up to *Roughing It in the Bush*. Although Moodie was puzzled by the fact that *Life in the Clearings versus the Bush* did not receive "a better hearing" in England, she could take consolation that the sales of and the critical response in the United States to *Mark Hurdlestone* were positive (*Susanna Moodie* 142). Capitalizing on the possibilities allowed under the copyright laws, the New York firm of DeWitt and Davenport had picked up *Mark Hurdlestone* and done very well by it. One of the publisher's newspaper advertisements reported that "over 10,000 copies have been sold within a week of publication." Moodie, however, received nothing from the success other than the promise from DeWitt and Davenport to pay her two hundred dollars "for the *first chance* of republishing my next work" (132). In the meantime, she sent to Bentley, not "another sober tale like *Mark*" (130), but an extensively rewritten version of her 1851 serial, "Trifles from the Burthen of a Life," the beginnings of her emigration story, which, though fictionalized,

was, she insisted, "no fiction" (131). Despite the weak showing of *Life in the Clearings versus the Bush* and "the abuse" she
felt that it had received, she was ready again to risk a critical
reaction in Canada in the hope that she might regain the
interest of British readers (135).

Moodie was fortunate in the personal consideration that
Richard Bentley extended to her. Although an astute busi-
nessman, he had developed a fondness for her that is reflected
in the openness of her letters to him and in the fact that the
Moodies welcomed his son Horace as a guest while he was
visiting Canada. When she cried poor in 1853, lamenting the
reduced state of John's income as sheriff (which she blamed
on the Belleville lawyers), Bentley again took a chance on her
writing, this time with what was now to be called *Flora
Lyndsay*. It appeared in 1854 in London, as did, late that same
year, *Matrimonial Speculations*, a volume comprised of three
previously published *Literary Garland* narratives: "Richard
Redpath," "Waiting for Dead Man's Shoes," and "The Miss
Greens." All were "comic stories" that she hoped might
please the English public better than her "sober" tales
(*Susanna Moodie* 151).

Even as Bentley published these two books, Susanna was
shifting her hopes to "Yankee" chutzpah and promised dollars. DeWitt and Davenport had bought the rights to *Roughing It in the Bush* from Putnam and the rights to *Life in the
Clearings versus the Bush* from Stringer and Townsend via
Harper and Sons. Moreover, the firm (associated in American politics with the "No-Nothing" or Nativist Party as
well as with the publication of cheap sensationalist books)
flattered her by asking to be her exclusive American publisher and by offering attractive terms (*Susanna Moodie* 150). As
a result, DeWitt and Davenport contracted with Bentley to
bring out both *Flora Lyndsay* and *Matrimonial Speculations*,
though bibliographical records suggest that the firm sub-

sequently decided not to publish the latter book in New York. Moodie reported to Bentley, however, that the American edition of *Life in the Clearings versus the Bush* had "a great sale" in both the United States and Canada, though she ruefully added that she had gained nothing by it (154). Fighting discouragement and confusion, but ready now to test the strength of her "large reputation" in America, Moodie therefore sought to reverse things to her own benefit by allowing DeWitt and Davenport to publish her next novel first. Thus, *Geoffrey Moncton; or, The Faithless Guardian* appeared first in New York in 1855 under the DeWitt and Davenport imprint; Bentley published it in London as *The Monktons* the following year. The American reviews were generally complimentary, but those in London were far from enthusiastic. The *Athenaeum*, with which Susanna had briefly been connected in 1830, dismissed it on 29 February 1856 as "a foolish novel," adding that "the characters and the story appear to have been brought out of a dusty toy-box" (qtd. in *Susanna Moodie* 112). When she heard from Bentley of its poor British sales, she concluded that, "with the British public, I can never hope to be a favorite" (*Susanna Moodie* 169).

The rush of book publishing that characterized the mid-1850s for Susanna Moodie followed the success of *Roughing It in the Bush*. No subsequent book (with the apparent exception of *Mark Hurdlestone* in the United States) so engaged public attention, and by 1855 it was becoming clear that she had reached an impasse for which she had neither any answer nor sufficient energy to address. Bentley had overextended himself on her behalf, and, when she sent him the manuscript of "The Linhopes" in 1856 (published originally as "The First Debt" in the *Literary Garland*), he turned it over to George Routledge for his consideration. Routledge eventually turned it down. It also appears that DeWitt and Davenport (about whose operations little is known) proved but a short-term support for her. While Moodie's letters are silent on the failure of that once promising New York connection, the depression that affected North America in 1857-58 may well have undermined DeWitt and Davenport's venturesomeness, if not its business. Late in 1858, Susanna told her sister Catharine that Horace Greeley had "undertaken to sell ["The Linhopes"] for [her] in the States." She was not optimistic, however, for "in these times — people want bread more than books. Authors have but a poor chance of success" (*Susanna Moodie* 185). Reporting to Bentley on the state of the colony's economy early in 1859, she commented on the widespread unemployment and the many failed businesses. "The Colony is bankrupt," she wrote, but it "cannot take the benefit of the insolvent act" (187). Although she had a great need for literary earnings at this period, her pen and her British and American connections failed her (178). Nevertheless, she continued half-hopefully to send manuscripts to Bentley, though nothing came of them.

The early 1850s were also a lively and demanding time in the lives of the Moodies' sons and daughters. Like many Canadian youths of his time, Dunbar, the eldest son, set out for California and Nevada to make his fortune. His letters home provided startling glimpses of that rough frontier world and a record of his disappointment in various mining claims. Although he soon returned to Belleville, his adventures awakened in him a desire to make his future elsewhere that could not finally be put to rest. A significant part of Susanna's literary earnings helped to support Donald, who, she worried, lacked "that energy which alone ensures success" (*Susanna Moodie* 189). Having run an educational gamut from apprenticeship in the law to medical studies at McGill, Donald was forced finally to return to Belleville from Montreal when the family finances reached a state of crisis in 1860. His laziness and drinking increasingly became matters of growing concern within the family. Rob(ert), meanwhile, moved from home education with his mother to schooling in Quebec until he too had to return home because of financial constraints. A reliable boy, he was a ready worker and the least of his parents' concern.

In August 1855, Susanna's eldest daughter, Katie, married John Joseph Vickers, an Englishman who had settled in Belleville and would go on to found the Vickers Express Company. But good marriages did not eliminate worry for the Moodies. Consumptive conditions plagued both Katie and Agnes, especially in relation to their childbearing. Agnes in fact lost a daughter in 1856, and in 1858 she was virtually penniless in Toronto despite her husband's law practice. Katie's health was so precarious in 1857 that the Moodies were advised to take her to the ocean to recuperate. On this occasion, Susanna herself was transformed from worry to delight, stimulated by the wonder of rail travel on the Grand Trunk line, the beauty of the New England scenery, the sight and feel — after so many years — of the ocean, and the agreeableness of the many Americans she met at Cape Elizabeth, Maine. Seeing the "grand hills of Vermont and New Hampshire" for the first time, she wrote that "my soul had gone into my eyes" (*Susanna Moodie* 176). She also sought to relieve Catharine's impoverished and difficult circumstances at Rice Lake by welcoming her sister and various of her children to Belleville for extensive periods. From Reydon, however, there was only silence; with much bitterness, Susanna reported to Richard Bentley in January 1856 that "They have ignored me and my books" (165).

Family finances began to pose a major problem when, in 1855, the continuing sequence of lawsuits brought against John Moodie as sheriff began to take their toll. In particular, the Cinq v. Mars case cost him heavily in time, worry, and money (*Susanna Moodie* 121). Susanna's anger with the Belleville lawyers, a consistent theme with her, boiled over in several letters. To Richard Bentley, for instance, she fumed against the "spider meshes of law and robbery" practised against her husband by calculating merchants and lawyers (178).

In 1858, however, John found himself in a much greater predicament, one from which he could find no settlement or escape. He was accused of and indicted for the crime of the farming of office. The charge had to do with the terms under which he had arranged to employ and pay his deputies, even though he had carefully sought legal advice before establishing the formal agreement that was the basis for the charge. Raging now against "the treachery of his advisors," who, having misinformed him, then testified against him, Susanna could foresee not simply reduced income but also the very loss of his position and reputation. John's increasing weakness and uncertain health, which had led her to urge him to take a holiday trip to Boston and New York in 1856, had become much more noticeable as he approached his sixtieth birthday, and he had begun more and more to rely on his deputies to look after the more demanding work of his office. A glance at the size of Hastings County on a map will make clear the huge area he was required to serve as sheriff.

What became for Susanna a kind of substitute for her writing and for John a relief from the burden and anxieties of his work was their growing passion for and commitment to Spiritualism in the latter half of the 1850s. An interest in the power and importance of intuition had long been evident in Susanna's writings. John, who saw himself as a rigorous rationalist, often teased Susanna about her emotional excesses and indulgences. The spiritualism movement, which they had been reading about and discussing with interest, presented itself to them in Belleville in the attractive person of Kate Fox. The youngest of the Fox sisters, or "the Rochester Rappers" as they were celebrated in the press, Canadian-born Kate was staying with her sister Elizabeth Ousterhout near Belleville in the summer of 1855 and visited the Moodies' home to provide a personal glimpse of the powers of spirits. Curious and fascinated, the Moodies thus became initiates to the mysteries of spirit communication and power.

For all his alleged resistance, John was quickly enthralled, while Susanna remained cautious and resistant. But the experimental séances at their home on Bridge Street and in the houses of a few like-minded Belleville friends soon drew her in, for she was an effective medium and a necessary participant in John's experiments. Thus, she was not long in becoming deeply committed to the "glorious madness" (*Susanna Moodie* 182). John himself had proved an unsatisfactory medium and rued that limitation. Instead, he treated the activity as much like a scientist as he could, deliberately recording the pertinent details of each séance and spirit communication, extending his reading and contacts, and seeking alternative means to facilitate contact with the spirit world. The Moodies even succeeded in interesting the visiting Catharine Parr Traill and their daughter Agnes in their séances. Agnes remained involved for years, but Catharine found her experiences as a medium so alarming that she soon distanced herself from the experiments (182).

As his enthusiasm grew, John became an increasingly active student of spiritualism and a committed proselytizer. He visited Toronto and New York in search of advice and guidance, and he sent his "Record(s) of Spiritual Investigations" and related letters and essays to a New York newspaper, the *Spiritual Telegraph*, in which they appeared from late 1857 to 1859. The initial letter was written as a response to William

Gregory, a professor of chemistry at the University of Edinburgh, whose book *Letters to a Candid Enquirer, on Animal Magnetism* (1851) had challenged the validity of certain popular parapsychological claims.

Readers interested in the details of the Moodies' involvement in the Spiritualist movement should consult *Susanna Moodie: Letters of a Lifetime* and *Letters of Love and Duty: The Correspondence of Susanna and John Moodie.* The latter contains several of John's letters to the *Spiritual Telegraph.* Drawing on the detailed entries in his diary, they document Susanna's participation as well as his engagement in the movement itself and in the related practice of hands-on healing. It is lamentable that the Moodies' conspicuous involvement in North American Spiritualism and their continuing contact with the Fox sisters (the Patrick Hamilton Ewing Collection contains one letter from Margaret Fox to Susanna) have been almost entirely overlooked by historians of the movement.

What can be said — from a distance at once sceptical and respectful — is that the Moodies' shared enthusiasm carried them over a number of difficult hurdles in their later life together, at least until 1863. Susanna's disappointments as a writer, John's continuing legal battle to preserve his position, his debilitating stroke in 1861, their adjustments to ageing and increasing physical weariness, and their ongoing struggles to make ends meet were reduced in significance by their participation in something they deemed grander and more consequential than the trials of daily life. Spiritualism thus became the last of Susanna's religious enthusiasms, her hope of a better life through the personal refinement of her spiritual capacities and the achievement of greater self-knowledge. Under its auspices, the Moodies became, as it were, their own spiritual arbiters; they believed that they were actually in contact not only with their dead parents,

Masthead of the *Spiritual Telegraph*

mentors, and friends but also with their lost children, particularly the much lamented Johnny. Consolation was not assured from such sources, but each contact held out a promise, and therein lay both the charm and the lure of continuing experimentation.

### REDUCED CIRCUMSTANCES/REDUCED POWERS

In their last decade together, the Moodies endured considerable disappointment and loss. Facing a greatly reduced income from John's office and less money from Susanna's writing, they were fortunate to find boarders in the Russell sisters from Jamaica. The two girls likely came to the Moodies via Catharine Parr Traill's old friend George Bridges, who had served as an Anglican minister in Jamaica and who sought to help their father, Robert Russell, find a respectable place in Canada for them. Lizzy "who is a daughter to me in my trouble" and "dear little Julia" were "both excellent young women" who seemed, to Susanna, "to have been sent to us in the most providential manner to lighten our distress" (*Susanna Moodie* 190). When John suffered the stroke that paralysed his left side in 1861, the income the sisters provided became all the more necessary. The Moodie household was further crowded when old Jenny Buchanan unexpectedly came "home," as it were, to die. In a touching letter to Catharine Parr Traill (28 December 1862), Susanna described Jenny's antic behaviour and horrible hygiene, making it clear that she understood why her old servant had returned and "meant to stay all the winter, as she enjoyed herself best where she was," rather than seeking out her real home and family (192).

Belleville proved to be at once the Canadian locale in which the Moodies lived the longest and yet another stage in their "untoward destiny" in Canada. Little wonder that in the late

Susanna and John Moodie, c. 1860.
COURTESY THE NATIONAL LIBRARY, OTTAWA.

1850s Susanna felt an increasing desire to leave the town
(*Susanna Moodie* 185, 188). As their eldest son was entertaining notions of taking up Horace Greeley's challenge and
moving to the western United States, she was inclined to
consider the possibility of accompanying him, though, when
faced with a firm opportunity, she typically fell back on her
characteristic resistance to change. Thus, the family limped
through the early 1860s on limited means, hoping against
hope that John might yet find some help in the courts even
as he was exhausting the possibilities of legal appeal. Finally,
on 15 January 1863, he formally resigned his office rather than
face the indignity of actual removal from it.

The advice John received was that by resigning he would
keep his name eligible for another government appointment. His resignation was received in Belleville and Hastings
County with much public regret and private affection, for
many people were convinced that he was not guilty of inten-
tional wrongdoing and that he had served the town well
during his long tenure as sheriff. A few months later (19 June
1863), perhaps not without coincidence, John made his last
entry in his spiritual diary, his passion for the "glorious
madness" apparently about to expire. Despite a specific
promise of help from no less a friend than John A. Macdon-
ald, no new appointment was offered to the elderly and
physically incapacitated former sheriff. A graceful retirement
from public life was thus his only consolation after the long
struggle.

The final blow for the ageing couple was the loss of their
stone house on Bridge Street in 1866. That loss had much to
do with their concern for the futures of their sons. Dunbar
had married the eldest of their Jamaican boarders, Lizzy
Russell, in March 1862, and they soon had two children.
By mid-decade, Dunbar and Lizzy were convinced of the
need to head south. They settled on Delaware as their goal.

Pressuring John and Susanna to help them make their dream a reality, they asked them to sell the Bridge Street home and go with them to the States. Having resisted for several years Dunbar's requests for special financial support, and having endured his accusations of their having favoured his younger brothers (both of whom had enjoyed better educational opportunities than he had), they finally — and foolishly — succumbed to his pressure. Ignoring the financial advice of John Vickers, whose sound counsel John had relied on for several years, as well as his daughter Katie's warnings about Dunbar and Lizzy, he decided to put the house, formerly secured in Susanna's name, in the hands of his son.

The decision proved disastrous. In their anger and disbelief, the Vickerses refused to speak to John and Susanna. Many were the accusations and recriminations, for the decision affected everyone in the family. With Dunbar and Eliza preparing to leave for a farm in Delaware, Susanna became seriously ill and was told by her doctors that she could not travel. By then, her own anger, which she now directed at Eliza more than at her son, was palpable. The girl who in 1860 had been "a daughter to me in my trouble" had become a "selfish, cold hearted arogant [sic] Quadroon," whose behaviour made it "impossible for us to live together" (223). Thus, entirely deprived of the major equity of their old age, the Moodies refused to leave Belleville. Rather, they moved into a small, rented cottage near the Bay of Quinte, where they lived until John's death in 1869. Such were their limited resources that they were little able to help Agnes Fitzgibbon and her six children when her husband died suddenly in 1865. Neither could they do much else than tap connections in the hope of helping their other sons. The resilient Rob, who married in 1863, did manage to stay employed for the most part, but Donald was a sadly different story. His laziness and indulgent habits (there were occasional newspaper reports about his being arrested for drinking and carousing) had become pronounced. Although he left for Brooklyn, where he worked briefly for old family friends, he married Julia Russell without his parents' consent in 1866 and was soon proving an unreliable husband. His later life would be a shambles, an ongoing cause of concern and regret for Susanna until her death.

Alone, much buffeted, but at least independent again, Susanna and John enjoyed their last three years together in the small cottage. In a letter written in December 1868 to her old Suffolk friend Allen Ransome, she described their modest but satisfying circumstances. Only Robert and Agnes among their five children came to see them there.

So here we are — living in a little cottage with just room enough to hold us, but beautifully situated on the edge of our lovely bay, with a fine common in front covered with noble trees through which we see the spires of Belleville about a mile distant, and for which we pay a rent of 12 pounds per annum and the rates 10 dollars. My servant Margaret's wages 12 pounds more for I am too old, now 65, for hard work and am able to earn the money that pays her wages. She is a good and faithful woman though *Irish* and a *Catholic*, and lived with us in our prosperity and will not leave us in age or poverty, and whom I regard as a tried and valued friend.

Then I have a faithful Skye terrier who is known by the name of Quiz, very ugly and small, but full of almost human intelligence and much more love than generally belongs to the dominant human race. A steel kitten Grim, who is dear M's especial pet. A perfect incarnation of mischief very common to the Maltese race. 24 hens who help to furnish our larder, who come to me to be fed at the sound of a small handbell. I had a favourite cow — y'clept Mrs. Powers but I was too poor to keep her, and had to sell her though the milk was a great comfort, M. living so much upon it. I have no garden — and I dearly love flowers and tending them, but I have learned like dear St. Paul to be content with little or to abound. (*Susanna Moodie* 245-46)

Both the Moodies returned in these years to writing as a resource. John sent poems and sketches home to the editor of the *Orkney Herald* in 1866 and 1867, and he collected his occasional pieces for what was his retirement project, a book entitled *Scenes and Adventures of a Soldier and Settler, During Half a Century* (1866), which was sold by subscription and earned him a surprising six hundred dollars (*Susanna Moodie* 245). Susanna supplied a few narratives to the short-lived *North American Magazine* in 1863-64, including the beginning of a new novel she entitled "Dorothy Chance." When the magazine failed, John Lovell, who had printed John Moodie's book, picked up the novel's serialization in one of his newspapers for the fee of one hundred dollars, allowing her to keep the copyright (238). Then Richard Bentley, with whom Susanna had resumed her correspondence, published the novel in three volumes as *The World before Them* (1867). Ever thoughtful to her needs, Bentley also initiated a petition to the Royal Literary Fund on her behalf. The RLF, a body founded to provide support for indigent authors and their families, awarded Susanna sixty pounds in the summer of 1865. Ironically, this was the only formal recognition she received in her lifetime from British or Canadian sources.

*The World before Them* merits brief consideration. Although Susanna joked that the initials of her heroine, Dorothy Chance, echoed those of the Dominion of Canada, the novel is quintessentially English. It was another of her noncontroversial "tales of a Canadian Winter Hearth" that had nothing to do with her adopted country. Yet in some ways it summarizes her career as a popular novelist, especially as it plays with certain plots, enthusiasms, social criticisms, and moral teachings. She enjoyed writing it, and she told Bentley that she thought he would like it better than any of the novels she had previously sent him.

Dorothy is a Suffolk foundling taken in as a baby by a hearty but trigger-tempered farmer named Lawrence Rushmore. Raised alongside Rushmore's son Gilbert, she is the subject of Gilbert's love. The father, however, refuses to approve the marriage, thus precipitating three volumes of episodic alienation and misadventure, particularly for the disappointed Gilly. Throughout the plot, the beautiful, black-eyed, good-hearted, industrious Dorothy, who seldom says a mean word about anyone and remains steadfastly loyal to those she loves even when they criticize and mistreat her, is the subject of much ill judgement, gossip, and abuse. For many years, her goodness is taken for granted or remains unrecognized, and she suffers many "great life-trial[s]" (1: 84). In the end, however, when the secret of her birth is pieced together and factually verified, she turns out to be the missing princess, the long-lost daughter of the local earl (Lord Wilton), whose terrible secret and personal losses have turned him from a nonchalant aristocrat to a melancholy but kindly patrician. Dorothy marries the Rev. Gerald Fitzmorris, a cousin of Lord Wilton, who having forsaken the excesses of the soldier's life for the ministry, has become an enthusiastic Christian dedicated to educating and helping the poor. With him, Dorothy assumes her rightful place of consequence but remains acutely mindful of the worth of humble life: indeed, "her chief delight was in doing good" (3: 309).

The novel iterates the extent to which Susanna Moodie was imaginatively driven by a plot of unrecognized worth and social position. As in *Geoffrey Moncton*, the setting is definitively English, rooted in a class system in need of invigoration and moral reformation from below. Her heroine neither rebels nor grumbles, despite her obvious worth, the injustices she endures, and her sense of mispositioning. Freighted with sentimentality and driven by melodramatic conflicts, the novel thus offers the satisfactions of an old-fashioned, Cinderella-like fable that is quintessentially middle class and moralistic in its vision. It is the unpretentious, hard-working, family-oriented Dorothy who, once the secret of her birth is clarified, is capable, in partnership with her reformed husband, of restoring order to the Old World and awakening the aristocracy to its proper role of paternalistic and, in Moodie's hands, Christian leadership. The extent to which this myth underlies her Canadian narratives is a subject perhaps for some future study.

*The World before Them* is, then, a deep bath in Susanna Moodie's Suffolk past. Just as John Moodie found himself exploring Celtic myths related to Orkney history and his family's roots in his late writings, Susanna turned away from Canada and its vexing social and political tensions. Although certain aspects of her longer life experience are evident in the novel — for instance, her continuing religious enthusiasm and her bristling contempt for women whose gossip and spite create misrepresentation, cruelty, and hatred in society — it is a work that virtually bypasses her Canadian experience. All that she had learned or suffered from in her Canadian life was set aside, and she fell back on the fables rooted in her childhood and girlhood. She was, as she told Henry Morgan in 1861, English "[b]y birth and education" (*Susanna Moodie* 191); the best she could be in Canada was "her daughter by adoption" (*Life* 280). The attempt to set herself up as a Canadian social critic and cultural spokesperson had cost her deeply. Having vowed to turn away from such painful self-exposure, she fell back on stories rooted in her beloved Suffolk countryside and her own reimagined, childhood view of a beloved, and almost entirely unrealistic, England.

CHAPTER 4

# Conclusion — *Alone Again*

When John Moodie passed quietly away in the early hours of 22 October 1869, a great deal of Susanna went with him. Surviving letters in which she describes his death are deeply moving. So too is her fortitude in her loss. Although she was lonely and looked ten years older, she resolved to keep up a brave face and never, as she put it, to shrink from her allotted task (*Susanna Moodie* 253). The happiness she had known in John's company simply could not be replaced.

More positively, John's funeral ended the inadvertent estrangement from the Vickerses, and Susanna found herself much in demand among her Canadian offspring. John Vickers again assumed the role of trusted financial advisor, and, building upon the properties left to her by her husband, he managed to keep her relatively comfortable during her remaining years. Although she left after the funeral to stay with Robert and his family in Seaforth, Ontario, where he was managing the Grand Trunk station, she soon returned to Belleville for a time, renting rooms in order to be near John's grave and her old friends. Gradually, however, Susanna drifted into a pattern of alternating between Rob's family in Seaforth (and later Weston, near Toronto) and Katie's family in Toronto. As often as possible in the 1870s, she spent her summers with Catharine Parr Traill, her daughter Kate, and

Catharine's granddaughter Katie at Westove, their cottage in Lakefield. When Agnes remarried the influential Colonel Brown Chamberlin of Ottawa in the early 1870s, Susanna attended the wedding; she stayed in close contact with Agnes, visiting her in Ottawa, where she achieved social prominence, and seeing her in Lakefield when Agnes began to summer there with children. In 1871, Agnes made a good sale of the Belleville building lots left to her by her father. With some satisfaction, Susanna noted that, when all was said and done, Agnes had done as well or better than her brother Dunbar as a result of John's precipitous redistribution of his holdings. Things turned out better than it had appeared they would in those rancorous days in 1866.

Susanna remained attentive to her older sons, though apparently she never saw either of them again. Catharine felt that her sister was doomed to be disappointed by her eldest boys, but Susanna kept up her hopes for them and did, in her last years, find some basis for hope in their letters to her.

Throughout the early 1870s, as Donald became increasingly alcoholic, Susanna heard very little from him. He usually wrote only when in need of money. Given his long silences, she constantly worried about his welfare and state of mind. By the mid-1870s, he had left Julia and his children. He was in fact a homeless and unemployed alcoholic, reduced to begging for money from his mother, other relatives, and friends. His condition, so apparently hopeless, caused her "terrible mental distress," but she sent him whatever money she could manage and urged him to seek help for his problem (*Susanna Moodie* 331). Finally, in Chicago late in the decade, he entered a "Home" and took the pledge, seeking to put his demons to rest. "His reformation would shed sunshine on my last days upon earth," Susanna told Catharine in 1879 (333). She was thus heartened to hear from him that he was

Vickers family, c. 1875.

holding down a job and attempting a reconciliation with his wife by the early 1880s.

Dunbar, who kept in contact with his parents despite the hostility between Susanna and his wife, reported in 1867 from Delaware that he did "not find it such an Eldorado as he expected" (*Susanna Moodie* 240). When his father died, Dunbar pleaded with Susanna, perhaps fed by a sense of guilt, to join them in Delaware. Disappointed by the fact that she chose to reside with Rob, his temper flared. Susanna reported the sequence of letters to Catharine in December 1869:

> He wrote to me very kindly, on receiving the news from Donald of his Father's death, and said that I *must* come to him, as it was with him I had to make my home. I answered him as soon as I was able, and gave him a full account of his father's death. But he wrote to me on my birthday. A very disagreeable letter, speaking most cruelly of his good brother, and going over all the old troubles. It was a sad affair altogether. I wrote to him in reply kindly and firmly, and refuted many things that I knew to be false, but he seems mad with jealousy that I preferred living with a younger brother to him. That letter upset me a good deal, for I have so truly repaid him good for evil, that it cut me to the heart, that he could write in such a strain to me, at such a time. But there must ever be a thorn in the flesh to keep us watchful, and I will not give him up yet. (271)

That correspondence did not, however, create the rupture Susanna seems to imply. In fact, she and Dunbar continued to write, and she followed the growth of his family and their movements — from Delaware to Colorado, and from farming to mining. She was most encouraged by his becoming first a temperance man and then, despite his stern and long-standing "infidelity," a Christian (*Susanna Moodie* 321).

The latter reformation occurred when two of his daughters died of peritonitis in 1882.

Her writing career clearly over, Susanna nonetheless harboured a few schemes and flirted with invitations to contribute to magazines while she wrote an occasional poem. One project she hoped to undertake — a collection of John's letters and a record of his life as a Canadian sheriff, which he himself had begun to work on — remained unfinished and, regrettably, seems to have vanished in the distribution of her papers among the family. She did, however, oversee the publication of the first Canadian edition of *Roughing It in the Bush* through the encouragement of her son-in-law John Vickers and his connection with George Rose of the Toronto firm of Hunter, Rose, and Company. Interestingly, Susanna also allowed it to be serialized in a Seaforth newspaper while she was boarding there with Rob's family. As well, she continued to paint for pleasure and the occasional sale, specializing in the flower arrangements that satisfied her inclinations and had been popular in the past.

She had long since abandoned Canadian subject matter as the basis for her writing. Only in her letters does one see how alive she was to the passing scene and how acute her skills of observation and description remained. In these she was able to make her personal experiences and ideas mean-ingful, resonant, and significant. She could express her excitement and emotional involvement with ease, con-fidently justifying her sudden shifts of mood as the most natural of reactions. "There is something in my character which always leads me to extremes," she confessed to Richard Bentley, a man who, though long hardened to the tempera-ments of writers, was much charmed by her letters. Then she added, with refreshing candour, "'From the sublime to the ridiculous,' as Napolean [sic] truly said, 'is but a step'" (*Susanna Moodie* 151). It was a step that she often took.

Above all, Susanna Moodie had the capacity to make herself fresh and lively; the vitality of her always youthful imagination never flagged, no matter how low her spirits fell, no matter how weary, worn, and buffeted she felt in her old age. It was that personalizing voice, the voice of a heart still young, the voice, finally, of a "wild Suffolk girl" in the body of an ageing Canadian woman, that informed her best writing, from *Roughing It in the Bush* through to *Flora Lyndsay* and her letters. After 1854, disillusioned and wounded by the Canadian responses she had aroused, she kept that personalized presence back, reserving it for her loved ones and her valued correspondents.

In the last two years of her life, that voice was silenced. Increasing dementia, perhaps the result of a stroke, perhaps of Alzheimer's Disease (Catharine Parr Traill called it "softening of the brain"), left Susanna in need of constant care, and she was confined to her room in the Vickerses' home at 152 Adelaide Street East in Toronto (*Susanna Moodie* 355). Catharine came down from Lakefield to be with her in late March 1885 and described her sister's condition in a letter. "What a strange change — what a wreck," she wrote (354). Noting several remarkable alterations in Susanna's habits, Catharine added, "This is to me the saddest sight for it shows the entire change that has come over her fine intellect — she is a child again in very truth. Poor dear old sister" (354).

On 11 April 1885, the end came. Susanna Moodie's "deranged state" and the "total loss" of "faculties" had reconciled her family to the inevitable. There were no last words at the bedside, no final glimpse of that "too active brain" that had made Susanna, at her best, a genius to Catharine (*Susanna Moodie* 355). "As she lay among the lilies and lovely flowers that in life were so dear to her," wrote Catharine to her daughter Annie, "I felt indeed that it was well that the toil and mental strife were over" (357).

Agnes (Moodie) Chamberlin, Moodie's second daughter.

REPRINTED FROM H.J. MORGAN, *TYPES OF CANADIAN WOMEN* (TORONTO, 1903).

# Works Consulted

Atwood, Margaret. *The Journals of Susanna Moodie*. Toronto: Oxford, 1970.

Ballstadt, Carl. "The Literary History of the Strickland Family." Diss. U of London, 1965.

Ballstadt, Carl, ed. *Roughing It in the Bush; or, Life in Canada* by Susanna Moodie. Centre for Editing Early Canadian Texts 5. Ottawa: Carleton UP, 1988.

"Secure in Conscious Worth: Susanna Moodie and the Rebellion of 1837." *Canadian Poetry* 18 (1986): 88-98.

Brown, Mary M. *An Index to The Literary Garland*. Toronto: Bibliographical Society of Canada, 1962.

____. *"The Literary Garland* and a Case of Literary Larceny." *Journal of Canadian Fiction* 2.3 (1973): 63-68.

Buss, Helen M. *Mapping Our Selves: Canadian Women's Autobiography*. Montreal: McGill-Queen's UP, 1993.

Ferguson, Moira. Introduction. *Prince* 1-41.

Freiwald, Bina. "The Tongue of Woman: The Language of the Self in Moodie's *Roughing It in the Bush." Re(dis)covering Our Foremothers: Nineteenth-Century Canadian Women Writers*. Ed. Lorraine McMullen. Ottawa: U of Ottawa P, 1990: 155-72.

Glickman, Susan. "The Waxing and Waning of Susanna Moodie's 'Enthusiasm.'" *Canadian Literature* 130 (1991): 7-26.

Harral, Thomas. *Selections from the Poems of the Late James Bird; with a Brief Memoir of His Life*. London: Simpkin, 1840.

Heilbrun, Carolyn G. *Writing a Woman's Life*. New York: Ballantine, 1989.

Jameson, Anna. *Winter Studies and Summer Rambles* 1838. Toronto: McClelland, 1990.

Kirkland, Caroline M. *A New Home — Who'll Follow? Glimpses of Western Life*. 1840. Ed. William S. Osborne. Masterworks of Literature. New Haven: Yale UP, 1963.

Langton, Anne. *A Gentlewoman in Upper Canada: The Journals of Anne Langton*. Ed. H.H. Langton. Toronto: Clarke, 1930.

Mitford, Mary Russell. *Our Village: Sketches of Rural Character and Scenery*. London: Whittaker, [1824-32].

Moodie, J.W.D. *Scenes and Adventures of a Soldier and Settler during Half a Century*. Montreal: Lovell, 1866.

_____. *Ten Years in South Africa*. London: Bentley, 1835.

Moodie, Susanna. *Enthusiasm, and Other Poems*. London: Smith, 1831.

_____. *Flora Lyndsay; or, Passages in an Eventful Life*. 2 vols. London: Bentley, 1854.

_____. *Flora Lyndsay; or, Passages in an Eventful Life*. New York: DeWitt, [1855].

_____. *Geoffrey Moncton; or, The Faithless Guardian*. New York: DeWitt, 1855.

_____. *Hugh Latimer: or, The School-Boys' Friendship*. London: Dean, 1828.

_____. *Life in the Clearings versus the Bush*. London: Bentley, 1853. Rpt. as *Life in the Clearings*. Ed. and introd. Robert L. McDougall. Toronto: Macmillan, 1959. Rpt. as *Life in the Clearings*. Afterword. Carol Shields. Toronto: McClelland, 1989.

_____. *Life in the Clearings*. New York: DeWitt, [1854].

_____. *The Little Prisoner: or, Passion and Patience*. London: Dean, n.d.

_____. *The Little Quaker; or, The Triumph of Virtue*. London: Cole, n.d.

_____. *Mark Hurdlestone; or, The Gold Worshipper*. 2 vols. London: Bentley, 1853.

_____. *Mark Hurdlestone; or, The Two Brothers*. New York: DeWitt, [1853].

_____. *Matrimonial Speculations*. London: Bentley, 1854.

_____. *The Moncktons*. London: Bentley, 1856.

_____. The Patrick Hamilton Ewing Collection. National Library of Canada, Ottawa.

_____. *Profession and Principle; or, The Vicar's Tales*. London: Newman, 1828.

_____. *Roughing It in the Bush; or, Life in Canada*. 2 vols. London: Bentley, 1852.

_____. *Roughing It in the Bush*. New York: Putnam, 1852.

_____. *Roughing It in the Bush; or, Life in Canada*. 2nd ed. 2 vols. London: Bentley, 1852. Toronto: McClelland, 1989.

_____. *Rowland Massingham: or, I Will Be My Own Master*. London: Dean, n.d.

_____. *The Sailor Brother; or, The History of Thomas Saville*. London: Dean, n.d.

_____. *Spartacus: A Roman Story*. London: Newman, 1822.

_____. The Susanna Moodie Papers. National Archives of Canada, Ottawa.

_____. *The World before Them*. 3 vols. London: Bentley, 1868.

[Warner, Ashton]. *Negro Slavery Described by a Negro: Being the Narrative of Ashton Warner, a Native of St. Vincent's.* Transcribed and ed. Susanna Strickland. London: Maunder, 1831.

Moodie, Susanna, and J.W.D. Moodie. *Letters of Love and Duty: The Correspondence of Susanna and John Moodie.* Ed. Carl Ballstadt, Elizabeth Hopkins, and Michael Peterman. Toronto: U of Toronto P, 1993.

———. *Susanna Moodie: Letters of a Lifetime.* Ed. Carl Ballstadt, Elizabeth Hopkins, and Michael Peterman. Toronto: U of Toronto P, 1985.

———. *Voyages: Short Narratives of Susanna Moodie.* Ed. and introd. John Thurston. Ottawa: U of Ottawa P, 1991.

———. *The Victoria Magazine, 1847-48.* Facsim. ed. Ed. and introd. W.H. New. Vancouver: U of British Columbia P, 1968.

Morris, Audrey. *Gentle Pioneers: Five Nineteenth-Century Canadians.* Toronto: Hodder, 1968.

Northey, Margot. "Completing the Self-Portrait: Moodie's 'Rachel Wilde.'" *Essays on Canadian Writing* 29 (1984): 117-27.

Peterman, Michael. "Susanna Moodie and Her Works." *Canadian Writers and Their Works.* Fiction Series, Ed. Robert Lecker, Jack David, and Ellen Quigley. Vol. 1. Toronto: ECW, 1983: 65-104. 12 vols. 1981-96.

———. "Susanna Moodie and Sir George Arthur: A New Letter." *Canadian Poetry: Studies/Documents/Reviews* 38 (1996): 130-38.

———. *"This Great Epoch of Our Lives": Introducing Roughing It in the Bush.* Canadian Fiction Studies 33. Toronto: ECW, 1996.

Pope-Hennessy, Una. *Agnes Strickland: Biographer of the Queens of England 1796-1874.* London: Chatto, 1940.

[Prince, Mary]. *The History of Mary Prince, a West Indian Slave, as Related by Herself.* Transcribed Susanna Strickland. 1831. Ed. Moira Ferguson. London: Pandora, 1987.

Pringle, Thomas. *African Sketches.* London: Moxon, 1834.

Ritchie, James Ewing. *East Anglia.* London: Clarke, 1883.

———. *To Canada with Emigrants.* London: Unwin, 1885.

Shields, Carol. *Susanna Moodie: Voice and Vision.* Ottawa: Borealis, 1977.

Strickland, Jane. *Life of Agnes Strickland.* Edinburgh: Blackwood, 1887.

Strickland, Samuel. *Twenty-Seven Years in Canada West: or, The Experiences of an Early Settler.* London: Bentley, 1853.

Thompson, Elizabeth. "An Early Review of *Roughing It in the Bush.*" *Canadian Literature* 131 (1996): 202-04.

Thurston, John. *The Work of Words: The Writing of Susanna Strickland Moodie.* Montreal: McGill-Queen's UP, 1996.

Traill, Catharine Parr. *The Backwoods of Canada: Being Letters from the Wife of an Emigrant Officer, Illustrative of the Domestic Economy of British America.* London: Knight, 1836. Rpt. as *The Backwoods of Canada.* Ed.

and introd. D.M.R. Bentley. Toronto: McClelland, 1989.

_____. *The Backwoods of Canada*. Ed. Michael Peterman. Centre for Editing Early Canadian Texts 11. U of Ottawa P, 1997.

_____. *Forest and Other Gleanings: The Fugitive Writings of Catharine Parr Traill*. Ed. Michael Peterman and Carl Ballstadt. Ottawa: U of Ottawa P, 1994.

_____. "I Bless You in My Heart." *Selected Correspondence of Catharine Parr Traill*. Ed. Carl Ballstadt, Elizabeth Hopkins, and Michael Peterman. Toronto: U of Toronto P, 1996.

_____. *Pearls and Pebbles; or, Notes of an Old Naturalist*. Toronto: Briggs, 1894.

The Traill Family Collection. National Archives of Canada, Ottawa.